WHY I AM A CHRISTIAN

Eric Heffer

WHY I AM A CHRISTIAN

Publisher's Note

Eric Heffer was able to complete this book before he died on 27th May 1991. Hodder and Stoughton are glad to publish it in his honour.

First published in Great Britain 1991

Spire is an imprint of Hodder & Stoughton *Publishers*

British Library Cataloguing in Publication Data

Heffer, Eric
Why I am a Christian.
I. Title
261.7

ISBN 0-340-55873-3

Printed in Great Britain for Hodder and Stoughton Limited, Mill Road, Dunton Green, Sevenoaks, Kent by Clays Limited, St Ives plc. Photoset by Rowland Phototypesetting Limited, Bury St Edmunds, Suffolk.

Hodder and Stoughton Editorial Office: 47 Bedford Square, London WC1B 3DP.

Dedication

FOR ELINOR

Contents

The human is articulated in man and woman, and thus occurs within a profoundly dialectical structure. The human being as such occurs, on the one hand, as what the anthropological sciences say he and she is; on the other hand, the human being is something not yet described or investigated – what we might call an open possibility. The human being is at once be-ing and being-able-to-be. The human being is the known and the unknown, the deciphered and the mysterious, the clear, the studied, the thought, the word, the order, the system – but also the silence that wraps that word, the darkness emitting the light, the chaos from which the astounding may emerge, the mystery that can ever be sketched in outline, but that ever remains mystery. The human being is the difficult dialectical unity of the two dimensions that constitute the human being – in the form of man and woman.

Leonardo Boff OFM, *The Maternal Face of God*

Foreword

Those who only knew Eric Heffer through his media image will find this book totally unexpected. Those of us who have shared with him in the struggle to stand up for Liverpool can truthfully say that we know better. Though even for us, or certainly for me, there is much that is new and profoundly moving in this statement of his personal 'credo'.

Writing in his diary in 1972, Tony Benn said of Eric Heffer that he was a freethinking man 'in the best non-conformist tradition'. As this book shows, ecclesiastically the comment is well off target as a description of somebody so strongly formed and influenced by the catholic tradition of the Church of England and by the powerful strands of Roman Catholic social concern. Yet at a deeper level, I think Tony Benn's remark captures the spirit of this book.

Eric Heffer followed his Christian faith and Socialist beliefs with a fierce personal integrity that left no authority unquestioned. He was not a comfortable member of a church or, I am sure, of a political party. But those (and I am one of them) who have crossed swords with him on occasions have always respected the unswerving loyalty and devotion to the most disadvantaged in our society that have motivated him.

In this fascinating book he reveals his vivid rediscovery of the suffering Christ while walking the Via Dolorosa, and his search for Christ's way in a suffering world. He speaks with refreshing openness about his own religious experience, the greatest influences on his life and faith, and of his firm attempts to hold together his Christian Socialism, both in the Labour Party and the Church of England. This heir of George Lansbury stands gloriously within such a tradition.

I remember a long Sunday evening, when Eric and Doris, his loyal and sensitive help mate, sat with us in our home in Liverpool: what struck me was his honesty about failures as well as successes of the Socialist movement, and his deep wish for the Church to be loyal to Christ's commitment to the poor. He continued to place many hopes in the Church and at the same time was quickly impatient with us. When I published a book with the title *Bias to the Poor*, he claimed me as an ally. He warmly supported the close ecumenical partnership in Liverpool between Archbishop Derek Worlock and myself. When we criticised the Militant leadership of the City Council, he attacked us for not giving them enough credit as 'working class lads'.

Eric Heffer was an intuitive Christian and politician: this book typically hits out at many targets. It lands right on the jaw quite often. In this personal statement of faith, written in the shadow of serious illness, they may see, as I do, authentic glimpses of Christ in the life of a whole-hearted champion of the poor.

David Sheppard
Bishop of Liverpool
June 1991

Preface

This short book outlines why I am a Christian and what I believe to be the Christian message. As far as possible, in the space available, I have endeavoured to deal with issues of war and peace and oppression and justice, the struggle for democracy in the Church, Christians who have affected my life and why I believe my Socialism is synonymous with my Christianity. I do not claim the book to be a great intellectual treatise, but it does outline why I believe that the Christian message of the New Testament, in particular, is basically a revolutionary message. It explains how Christ stood four-square with the poor and how in essence Christianity is a poor man's religion. I also say why Christ is a force for the liberation of mankind. I further reveal how in 1968 in Israel I had a remarkable religious experience which has had a profound effect on my life.

I realise that my views will not be popular with everyone, certainly not with some Conservatives who believe that Christianity should not get mixed up with politics, and that the emphasis of the Church should be on personal salvation. If one studies the New Testament carefully then clearly it is God's Kingdom here on earth we have to work for, and that surely means the liberation of mankind from the evils of the society in which we live.

Eric Heffer

Chapter 1

Background in the Church

> Faith is no more or less than man's historical activity (which is essentially political). In seeking the basic meaning of his historical existence, man goes so deep into his human 'why' that he comes up against the mystery of God working in history, but never outside it.
>
> Hugo Assman, *Practical Theology of Liberation*

Two things have prompted me to write this short book. Firstly, a recent book *Christianity and Conservatism*, edited by Michael Alison MP and David L. Edwards; and secondly, the fact that for some years I have frequently discussed the question of why I am a Christian with a journalist friend and have tended to dodge giving her a clear answer.

My friend has serious worries about believing, yet is genuinely concerned, telling me she appreciates my acceptance of Christianity far more than she does my

Socialism. What I want to convey is that my Christianity and my Socialism are synonymous. The one stems from the other.

The first point I would seriously make is that believing in Christianity does not necessarily mean accepting everything in the scriptures, in the sense that every word must be believed and every miracle considered true. For some people, miracles can too easily be proved historically incorrect and ridiculed by writers and historians hostile to religion.

I think it was in Cardinal Newman's *Apologia Pro Vita Sua* that he argued that miracles could not be accepted as happening only in the days of Christ, but ought to be accepted at any time, and not rejected in modern society as they were by many Protestant theologians. There could be no half-way house miracles; either they took place or they did not.

At the time of reading the *Apologia*, I was deeply impressed by Newman's argument that there was no middle way. But I drew the conclusion that miracles in fact never took place, that they were mythology. His argument joined my arsenal of opposition to religion, part of my atheism.

Today, I am sure I was wrong. There have been plenty of examples of miracles in modern times, and although the Church authorities are right to be cautious and sceptical, miracles do occur and will, at certain times, continue to occur.

Over the years, at various times in church, I have enjoyed the ritual, loved the hymns, generally liked the service and then been put off by the banality and sometimes the stupidity of the sermon, realising that the 'Christianity' being preached had nothing to do with what I believed Christianity to be.

Early beliefs

Like most British people of my age, I was born into a Christian family. Church was an accepted part of our being. It was not questioned. It was as natural as breathing the air. I attended church (Church of England) three times on a Sunday and often during the week, went to Sunday school and was in the choir. I sang at weddings and funerals and of course attended choir practice. The church was a natural and essential part of my life.

For Christmas and birthday presents I received from my grandmother and others the Bible, the Book of Common Prayer, the Psalms and books such as *Pilgrim's Progress*, and others about our missionaries converting and 'civilising' the 'heathens' in Africa and Asia.

I learned the Ten Commandments, I chanted the Creed. I sang the Magnificat and listened to the words of the Sermon on the Mount. Slowly, the real and true message of Christianity was penetrating my thoughts. It was not only the acceptance of Christ as a revelation, as the Son of God, but an acceptance of the idea that one can believe this; because the world was not perfect, people were not perfect and we should work to make people better and the world a better place to live in – 'Thy Kingdom come on earth, as it is in heaven'.

At that stage of my life I had not read any of the works of the early Church Fathers. The lives of the saints were unknown to me. All that came later, after I had stopped going to church and had become what I thought was an atheist.

Cardinal Newman, however, was certainly known to me. My mother had a number of pictures and prayers framed and hung on the walls of our house, and Newman's 'Lead, kindly Light' was very prominent among them. Clearly, Newman was accepted in my home because he had been an Anglican priest, later moving on to the Roman Catholic Church.

It should be remembered that our Creed says, 'I believe in the holy catholic Church, the communion of saints, the forgiveness of sins.' I was therefore a Catholic, not a Protestant; I never really liked the services of the more Protestant sections of the Church of England, and as a boy never set foot in a Congregational, Baptist or Methodist church, a Quaker meeting house or Bethel chapel. I did, however, often attend the Roman Catholic church. Again, the Catholic teaching of the Church of England was as natural to me as living itself. Not that I fully understood it. I did not. It was only later that I began to fully understand the arguments about transubstantiation, the 'real presence' as against the 'spiritual presence', and so on. By then I had more or less turned my back on all religions and read about these questions purely out of interest and because I had an enquiring mind and wished to know why things happened and why people believed in religion or philosophy.

Adult faith

I can hear my journalist friend saying, 'Yes, I know about your childhood, you have told me, but what about your belief in God? Why do you believe, and why are you a Christian? Stop dodging and weaving. Answer the question honestly.'

The truth is, it is a difficult question. I do believe there is a God, my heart tells me so; but sometimes, often, my head argues differently and therefore I cannot come out with a pat answer. The issue is far more complex than that.

Life is a great mystery and it is that mystery which is at the heart of the matter.

Margaret Thatcher, in her preface to *Christianity and Conservatism*, hits the nail on the head when she describes how 'the Herodians and the Pharisees conspired together to trap Jesus . . . so as to secure his arrest and execution. So great was the imagined political threat which Christ represented, that two groups – not normally on the same side – made common cause to try to do away with him.'

The facts are, he was not an imagined threat, he *was* a threat, and the Herodians and Pharisees in collusion with the Roman authorities did away with him. He was crucified, and there is no doubt he died for us. He was a revolutionary. He wanted to change society. For that he could not be forgiven – and the 'crucifixion' of such people continues to this day. Just look around our world. Look at El Salvador, Honduras, various African countries and parts of Asia, where those who side with the poor as Christ did are 'done away with'.

Recently, I read a novel by Howard Fast, *The Confession of Joe Cullen*. The story is about a helicopter pilot, an ex-Vietnam veteran, of Roman Catholic Irish origin, who took a job flying weapons into Honduras to be used by the Contras, bringing out drugs in payment. In the process he saw Father Francis Luke O'Healey murdered, dropped from the helicopter he was flying, after which he could not live with himself. The Irish priest, who sided with the poor, was a 'Liberation Theologian'. In the book, Fast makes Father O'Healey say:

> We are the children of God, I have never doubted that, but I do doubt that pain and suffering among the rich can never be measured against pain amongst the poor . . . Thus I see the mission to the poor and the oppressed as being the highest calling to which a priest can aspire; and if the poor are oppressed and if their condition derives from their oppression, must a priest abandon them? Can he still

minister to them and not be part of their struggle against the oppression?

This concept of the role of a Christian priest challenges the belief that the Christian religion teaches that a person's life on earth is only the prelude to the future life to come in heaven. It is a view of Christianity – that is, that the life hereafter is the thing to strive for – which I cannot accept. If the idea is to create heaven on earth, then it is the condition of the living people that we as Christians must be concerned with. It is the life they live now which is all-important, and not some afterlife that may or may not be wonderful, or which may or may not even exist.

I have never liked the idea that if one sins, one will personally end up in hell, suffering eternal physical torment. The fact is, for millions of people hell exists here on earth. Torment is real, they experience it every day. It is the elimination of that torment that we as Christians should be concerned about, not its perpetuation in an afterlife.

The concept of sin

What precisely is sin? Near to my home in Hertford, across the river from our house, lived a family who were members of one of the extreme Protestant sects. There were three boys and one girl, and on Sundays we could hear them singing their hymns and if we passed by their window we could see them clustered around a small organ in religious fervour. The lives of the children were totally repressed. The regime they lived under was oppressive. In essence they were tortured by their parents, who believed that such repression would rid their children of their innate propensity to sin.

If one accepts that sexual intercourse leading to illegitimate children was sin, then the girl eventually sinned, as did the boys, and the efforts of their parents came to nothing.

The threat of hell-fire and damnation did not succeed. In fact, the very repression suffered by the children led to the opposite results. How much better it would have been had they had a more liberal life and been told properly about birth control and that sex is not evil but natural, and best if love, real love, is involved.

Today, the Church, Catholic and Protestant, is undergoing a renewal. It is finding its way back to the fundamental teachings of Christ and slowly but surely becoming Christian again. This will not be easy; it could well be a fairly long process, and real tensions, perhaps further splits, may take place. But it will happen because the circumstances of life demand it.

In the summer of 1983, I was given a book by Father Fitzgerald of St Francis de Sales, Walton, in Liverpool. It was written by Father Austin Smith, a Passionist priest in Toxteth, Liverpool, and was called *Passion for the Inner City*. In my copy of the book Father Fitz, as we call him, had written, 'Towards a new society where compassion is a priority'. That is the essence of Christian thinking.

In Austin Smith's book, with its options for the poor, he writes, 'The cry of the poor in our times is not merely a summons into new activity, it is a demand that we radically change our lives.' He goes on to say, '. . . unless we agree to hear in the depths of our hearts the cry of the oppressed, a hearing which will call each one of us, in all differing ways, "to exist with and suffer with" the powerless. If we do not do so with some urgency, we shall betray the wonder of God's creation.'

Earlier in the book, Austin stresses that 'community is the epiphany of creation.' He warns, however, that 'personal and structural selfishness is always waiting to ambush those who would attempt such a vision.'

He could have been writing of what Margaret Thatcher said in a speech in 1988 to the General Assembly of the Church of Scotland, when she declared:

> In our day the only way that we can ensure that no one is left without sustenance, help or opportunity, is to have laws to provide for health and education, pensions for the elderly, succour for the sick and disabled. But intervention by the state must never become so great that it effectively removes personal responsibility. The same applies to taxation, for while you and I would work extremely hard whatever the circumstances, there are undoubtedly some who would not unless the incentive was there. And we need *their* efforts too.

That really sums up the difference between those who preach and understand the Christian religion and those who do not, but often say they do.

Chapter 2

Vision in Jerusalem

> Now I bid you consider that that face so ruthlessly smitten, was the face of God himself; the brows bloody with the thorns, the sacred body exposed to view and lacerated with the scourge, the hands nailed to the cross, and afterwards, the side pierced with the spear; it was the blood, and the sacred flesh, and the hands, and the temples, and the side, and the feet of God himself, which the frenzied multitude then gazed upon.
>
> Cardinal John Henry Newman,
> *Parochial and Plain Sermons*

The film about the life of Christ that in my opinion can never be bettered is Pier Paolo Pasolini's *The Gospel According to Saint Matthew*. In October 1962, awaiting with friends a visit from Pope John XXIII, Pasolini was a guest in Assisi of the Cittadella, established by Don Giovanni Rossi, and whilst there he read the Gospels. He said he had not read them for twenty years or so, but when he read them through like a novel, he felt 'an immediate need to "do something" – a terrible almost physical energy' and was, he said, overcome by an 'increase in vitality'.

As a Communist he still did not believe that Christ was the Son of God, but he believed that Christ was divine: '. . . I believe, that is, that in him humanity is so lofty, strict, and ideal as to exceed the common terms of humanity.' For me, Pasolini says it all. The feeling may be irrational, emotional, but it is there. Pasolini dedicated his film to Pope John XXIII.

An experience of God

Like Pasolini, for years, as a Communist, and then as a Socialist, I did not believe, or thought I did not. Then I went to Israel in 1968 and visited the Church of the Holy Sepulchre. I walked along the Via Dolorosa almost as in a trance. Here was the path that Christ had trodden, persecuted every inch of the way. The crown of thorns, the Cross became real. I could see in my mind's eye the agony of Christ, the suffering he carried for the poor. He was to be crucified because of his love for them. Among the people who watched this, some as always were mistakenly glad, others suffered with Christ every inch of his painful path. I could see it all. It was as if I was at the crucifixion itself, and all my early beliefs came flooding back. I felt bathed in a bright light and Christ was saying to me, 'Come with me, we are on the same side. I fought in my day for what you believe in today. I am the son of God, you must help to secure God's Kingdom.'

I remember going into the church, rejecting much of the attitudes of the clergy of the various denominations who looked after the church but did not show any great love for it. To me they were irrelevant. I knew that

Christ had been right, and since that time I have never really had any doubts.

I am sure my atheist friends and others will say, 'A likely story! It's pure fantasy. He must have suffered delusions.' I don't know. All I know is that it happened and I again became a believer. In his own way, so too did Pasolini, because his film is the most wonderful religious film I have ever seen.

Why did I not proclaim my experience from the house-tops? I'm not really sure, except that because I was an MP I feared I would not be believed and there would be those who would accuse me of looking for publicity or pulling some kind of political stunt. All I would say was that I had become a Christian believer again, but that it was a personal thing. I had no intention of speaking publicly about it or writing about my experience. It was some years before I spoke about my Christian concepts and gave lectures or wrote anything serious.

All my wife knew was that clearly I had changed, that I went to church on occasions and that I was now a believer.

There were occasions when I was interviewed on television, and although I proclaimed my Christian views, I was more than cagey about the experience I had undergone in the Holy Land. My main thrust was my politics, my Socialism, but increasingly, I related my political views to my Christianity.

The interesting thing is that over the years I had maintained an interest in religious affairs. I had read widely about the Christian Socialists from the earliest days to the present time.

Even in my 'atheist' days I would sometimes go to church services when I attended conferences and so on, and I certainly visited churches regularly to sit and contemplate in quiet, noting those in prayer. I never really understood why I did this. It was as if I was drawn to the Church by a great magnet over which I had no control.

Faith – private and public

After my clear re-acceptance of God I began to pray again, mainly to ask for strength and for guidance in the fight against oppression, for justice and peace.

I could not, however, accept many of the Church's concepts. At first they appeared to me to be sheer superstition. Some still do. What was central to my acceptance of Christianity was the crucifixion, i.e. the Cross. The Cross is the real symbol of Christianity. It is the Cross of oppression. It expresses the condition of the poor, but equally, because of Christ's agony and suffering, the hope of the world. Through the Cross a new society, God's Kingdom, can be created, and a new world of justice and peace built.

It has to be admitted that, in the past, the Cross has also, in the wrong hands, been a symbol of oppression, of imperialism, of extreme nationalism, of discrimination and intolerance. As always in society, the path of straightforward decency and righteousness has not been simple and clear.

The Christian religion has constantly been obliged to renew itself, both within the Roman Catholic Church and the Orthodox Church, and in the various breakaways, such as the Anglican Church and the many forms of Protestantism. After the early beginnings, the Church turned away from being the Church of the poor. It too often became the state religion, and from being the champion of the people it at times turned into their oppressor, becoming the instrument of the rich and privileged in society against the poor. It was this negative side which we 'atheists' played up. We equated the Inquisition in Spain with the Church. We emphasised the sectarianism and intolerance, and to a large extent we ignored those Christians in all sections of the Church who continued to believe in the basic ideas of Christ, siding with the poor and working to build a new world – those who were wrongly called heretics, when in fact they were the true heirs of Christ, who continued to work and fight for his ideas.

It seemed as if the political struggles were played out in the form of religious struggles. That was true up to a point, but the ideas and beliefs of those involved were underplayed, as if the politics of the class struggles were an end in themselves, when in fact they were not. The deep religious conviction held by those involved had a life apart from the political organisations.

Let me hasten to say that those who profess Christianity are not necessarily better people than those who are not. Some who reject religion in its entirety lead good and decent, exemplary lives. They are compassionate and against oppression, they are for justice and peace and would give their very lives to ensure that their beliefs are put into practice.

Some are saintly, genuinely so, whilst others who profess Christianity seem to be the total opposite of all that Christ believed in and stood for. Some so-called Christians are, in fact, bigots, intolerant and oppressive in their attitudes. If there were such a thing as the eternal fires, they would probably spend their time in them after death, whilst I am sure that many who profess 'atheism' and who publicly reject religion and God might be happily accepted into heaven.

Again, it depends upon what we mean by goodness. What are the criteria? Unctuous, creepy sentiments, the 'I am better than thou' syndrome, the goody-goody view of society, surely cannot be the criteria, because too much hypocrisy is involved. This has been proved beyond doubt, especially in the USA, where some of the new Right, 'born-again' Christians have proved to be crooks, fornicators, drug pedlars and generally silver-tongued rotters of the first order.

The evidence for this has been detailed in television programmes and also in the book by Sara Diamond, *Spiritual Warfare – The Politics of the Christian Right.* The book deals particularly with the USA, Latin America and South Africa. As I do not wish to be misunderstood, I hasten to add that not all 'born-again Christians' are in the same category as those I am criticising. The contribution of thousands of Evangelicals and others who consider themselves 'born again' cannot be faulted, and is important to the Church. Christianity must be all-embracing, with all sects and denominations making their own particular contribution to the Christian faith.

Christians who took the side of the Contras were not only from among the Protestants. Catholics too were involved, and both sections of the Church have created their own right-wing political groups.

Some 'born-again' Christians preach personal salvation, individualism and that the capitalist system is the best of all possible worlds. In Latin American countries they are often financed or assisted by the CIA, becoming the instrument of authority against the people. They too often side with the 'powers that be' and excuse the actions of the death squads which, in countries like El Salvador, are used to kill Catholic priests and nuns as well as other church workers; people who have sided with the poor and accepted the concepts of Liberation Theology.

Liberation Theology

Today, Catholic priests, particularly in Latin America, but not only there, are seeking to live Christianity by living the life of the peasants and urban poor.

I have given the example of Austin Smith, the Passionist priest in Toxteth, living and working among Liverpool's urban poor. He follows the example of those priests in Central and Latin America who have often given their lives for Christ's teachings. Some have gone further and actually joined in armed struggle against the oppressors. The most famous of these was Camilo Torres, the young Colombian ex-priest, who in the Colombian village of Patio Comonte was shot by government troops on 15th February 1966.

Torres came from a rich Colombian bourgeois family. Like young people so often do, he had gone to the extreme and died in the struggle. Others never preached violence or involved themselves in it, yet they too have died for the simple 'crime' of believing in and trying to carry out Christ's teaching. A recent BBC TV film on El Salvador, about Archbishop Romero and others who were murdered, showed clearly how the authorities and the rich of that country considered the Church, especially Jesuit priests, to be a menace because of their teachings of Christ's views.

What then are Christ's teachings? We should recall the words of the Magnificat, once described as 'the hymn of the universal social revolution' and as 'the inspired summoning of the tendency and direction of the future history of humankind':

> He hath shewed strength with his arm: he hath scattered the proud in the imagination of their hearts.
>
> He hath put down the mighty from their seat: and hath exalted the humble and meek.
>
> He hath filled the hungry with good things: and the rich he hath sent empty away.
>
> (Luke 1:51–53)

That is a very clear view of what Christ really stood for. We should remember that he drove the moneylenders from the Temple, that he argued that it would be easier for a camel to go through the eye of a needle than for a rich man to enter the Kingdom of Heaven. He turned water into wine at a wedding, and fed the masses from a few loaves and fishes.

Leonardo Boff, in his *Jesus Christ, Liberator*, argues that the Kingdom of God implies a revolution of the human world. He points out that Christ denounced the 'perfect', people 'who were not like the rest of men who could be grasping, unjust, adulterers and tax evaders . . . they observed fasts and paid taxes on all they got' (Luke 18:11,12) and who so appreciated religion that they built holy monuments. He said, despite all this, 'You have neglected the weightier matters of the law – justice, mercy, good faith . . . These you should have practised, without neglecting the others' (Matthew 23:23).

In my view, Leonardo Boff proves beyond doubt that Jesus was free from preconceived ideas and gave himself to others, especially those abandoned physically and mentally. He says, 'This world as it is, cannot be the location of the Kingdom of God. It must suffer a restructuring of its very foundations. It is love that saves, the disinterested acceptance of others and the complete opening of self to God.' He quotes the words of Carlos Mesters:

> It is not for us to judge others, defining them as good or bad, faithful or unfaithful, since the distinction between good and evil people disappears, if you are good to others. If evil people exist, then examine your conscience. You have closed your heart and have not helped others to grow. The misery of this world is neither an excuse nor a motive for flight, but an accusation against yourself. It is not you who should judge misery, but misery judges you and your system and makes you see its defects.

Such a view is the very opposite of that which argues that unemployment is the fault of the unemployed; that drug addicts are themselves totally responsible for their addiction; that the poor are responsible for their poverty and that the rich are rich because they deserve to be and the poor are poor because they are shiftless and are not prepared to 'pull their fingers out'.

As I said earlier, the Cross and the crucifixion are the symbols of Christianity. The central feature of Christian worship is the Mass, Eucharist, Holy Communion or the Lord's Supper or whatever it is called in the various Churches. It means our acceptance of the fact that we are all brothers and sisters to each other, that we must share in each others' joys and anxieties, care for each other, and particularly care for those who are unable for whatever reasons to care for themselves. Sharing in the Eucharist means we are all part of each other. We are our brothers' and our sisters' keepers, and because of that, we must have the vision of building and creating a new, compassionate society which ends poverty and misery for the many, and where justice and peace prevail.

Chapter 3

Socialism and Christianity

> I am a Church of England clergyman – and I am a Chartist
>
> The Rev. Charles Kingsley at a meeting, 23rd April 1849

I said earlier that my Socialism was synonymous with my Christianity. Let me explain in greater detail what I mean by that.

When I was young, I heard Conrad Noel, the vicar of Thaxted, preach the revolutionary message of Christianity. Noel's message was based upon his readings at theological college of the early Fathers of the Church. He discovered that they held revolutionary opinions on usury and private property as well as on the oppression of the poor by the rich. He said he 'compared socialism with the Gospels and contrasted them both with the contemporary commercial individualism which kills the body, and the theological individualism which casts both body and soul into hell'.

Noel joined the Guild of St Matthew, led by Stewart Headlam, and in the political field he joined the Social Democratic Federation. Both, to some extent, were dogmatic.

The Guild, however, was not viewed with enthusiasm by some churchmen because it sided with the rationalists in their fight to remove the blasphemy laws. But it also debated with the rationalists, arguing that they were distorting Christian teaching, its origins and so on. It set against the rationalists the teaching of Christ and the early Church, and developed the ideas of social Christianity.

Stewart Headlam urged the Church to 'let the people see that the Christian Church is the great secular society, that the Kingdom of which Jesus spoke was not merely a place to which people go hereafter but a divine society established in this world.' Headlam was a bold man. He spoke about 'the Christian Communism of the Church of the Carpenter . . . a baptised brotherhood of equals . . . distinctly and essentially democratic'. He said of Jesus that he was

> a Carpenter who became a Radical reformer both in social and economic matters . . . the social and political emancipator, the greatest of all secular workers, the founder of the great Socialist society for the promotion of righteousness, the preacher of a revolution, the denouncer of Kings, the gentle, tender sympathiser with the rough and the outcast, who could utter scathing, burning words against the rich, the respectable, the religious.

These statements made by Conrad Noel and Stewart Headlam are statements of both Christians and Socialists. They did not see any basic contradiction between Christianity and Socialism. For them the Gospels, the word of God, was essentially the Socialist message. I fully agree with that.

Christ and power

The Church, since its earliest days, and after it was taken over as the state religion, has always had two basic trends. There have been those who have accepted authority and power, and in the process have ignored Christ's basic ideas, and those prepared to continue to fight for his ideas, as expressed in the words of Stewart Headlam.

Conrad Noel was the most influential of the Christian Socialists. He argued passionately that Christ wanted to establish God's Kingdom on earth, modelled on the ideal Kingdom as it was formulated in God's mind. He argued that such a Kingdom would be based on divine justice, with the holding in common of the land and of capital.

It was Noel's view that the liturgy was soaked in Socialism. He argued that the Church of England, in taking its stand at the Reformation on not only the Bible but the Bible as interpreted by the early Church Fathers, was therefore committed to Communist/Socialist principles which went well beyond the modest proposals put forward by the then existing Socialist parties.

His view was that too often the Church had abandoned or gone against its own founding principles, but that throughout the ages there had always been people in the Church who had remained faithful to the traditions of social catholicism, to the gospel of social righteousness.

Whilst Conrad Noel and many others who were Christian Socialists were Anglo-Catholics, Christian Socialism was by no means confined to the Catholics in the Church of England. The social gospel was preached by others, some in the Methodist Church, and in the various dissenting churches like the Congregationalists and the Baptists.

At one stage, a Labour Church Movement was formed. The leading individual was John Trevor who left his Unitarian pulpit to form what some called a 'Socialist Salvation Army'. That was in 1891.

Labour Churches

The Labour Churches formed a Labour Church Union which drew up a set of principles:

1. That the Labour Movement is a Religious Movement.
2. That the Religion of the Labour Movement is not a class religion, but unites members of all classes in working for the abolition of communal slavery.
3. That the religion of the Labour Movement is not sectarian or dogmatic but Free Religion, leaving each man free to develop his own relations with the power that brought him into being.
4. That the Emancipation of Labour can only be realised so far as men learn both the Economic and Moral Laws of God, and heartily endeavour to obey them.
5. That the development of personal character, and the improvement of social conditions are both essential to man's emancipation from moral and social bondage.

It was in the Labour Churches that the emancipation of women as a principle was given voice to. It should be remembered that until the granting of women's suffrage, politics was seen as men's business. Dorothy Scott, writing in the Labour Church paper, *Labour Prophet*, in February 1892, said about women, 'They do care; they do want to know all about these unions and Eight Hour Bills, and competition and such like, and they want to have the chance of hearing your Tom Manns and Ben Tilletts, and if you'll let them come along, side by side with you, life will be ten times better.'

It is interesting to note that Stewart Headlam, Conrad Noel and Percy Dearmer, all Anglo-Catholics, spoke regularly at Labour Church meetings. Naturally, they had some differences with the leaders of the Labour Churches, whose emphasis was on individual religion, whereas Noel and the others placed greater emphasis on the Catholic social teaching as the religion of Socialism.

I am sure that, had I been around then, I might well have occasionally attended Labour Churches, but I would have been much more attracted to the traditional Anglican churches of an Anglo-Catholic hue. The Social Catholicism of Noel, Headlam and Dearmer would have been my forte, as it still is.

The growth of the Labour and Trade Union movements in the advanced industrial world undoubtedly had its effect on the main Churches, including the Roman Catholic Church. Pope Leo XIII, in December 1878, issued *Quod Apostolica*, which strongly attacked Socialism. In that encyclical, he said that Socialism attacked 'all that has been wisely decreed by human and divine laws for the protection and advancement of life'. He said the Socialist idea of equality was wrong: 'They wish to snatch away and hold in common all that has been acquired by legitimate inheritance, by labour of brain or hands, and by economy.'

Some years later, in May 1891, Pope Leo XIII issued an even more famous encyclical, *Rerum Novarum*. It was from this that the Roman Catholic social teaching grew. He argued in the encyclical that the Church must speak out, remedies had to be found to a situation in which labouring people found themselves little better off than in slavery, defenceless against the rapacity of callous employers. He continued to oppose the Socialist solution. At the same time he spelled out a 'Great

Charter for Labour', which would protect the worker from the 'cruelty of men of greed'.

He argued that there should be working men's associations, i.e. trade unions. He said these could 'shake off courageously the yoke of . . . intolerable oppression'.

It was clear that *Rerum Novarum* was intended to offset Marx's *Communist Manifesto*. It did not, however, succeed in doing that; but it did begin the process towards today's Liberation Theology. It ignored the early teachings of the Church, but because it pointed to some extent in the same direction, it was only a matter of time before those influenced by Catholic social teaching went the whole way, back to Christ's principles. That is what has happened.

Christian trade unions

One of the most important aspects of *Rerum Novarum* was that it encouraged workers to create, independently, their own organisations; and all over the world Catholic trade unions were formed which were no less militant in their actions than those unions which were not Roman Catholic.

The attitude of Pope Leo XIII with regard to trade unions has been developed over the years. In Italy, there are three trade union centres, unlike Britain where there is only one. The Catholic centre of unions in Italy is known as CISL (*Confederazione Italiana dei Sindacati Liberi*). For many years I wrote for a trade union journal in Italy run by the Socialist/Communist unions. What I found interesting was that the Socialist/Communist Unions (CGIL – *Confederazione Generale Italiana dei Lavoratori*) collaborated with the CISL, and together they often called strikes taking joint action. Here in this country, a year or so ago, the Catholic Truth Society issued a pamphlet on the rights of workers in unions, which, as I said in the House of Commons, was better than the policy being advocated by the Labour Party which, to some extent, is a pale reflection of Conservative policy.

The Catholic Truth Society pamphlet was very keen on the right to strike and believed that present Tory government policy had taken away one of the workers' fundamental rights.

The CTS pamphlet was clearly an extension of *Rerum Novarum* and reflects the new thinking taking place within sections of the Roman Catholic Church, thinking which I find very heartening and, as I said earlier, a step by the Church towards traditional Christianity.

When one looks back on history, one can see that there were always groups in the Church who fought valiantly for Christ's ideas. For example, in England during the 1381 Peasants' Revolt, there were Christians like John Ball, the hedge priest, who sided totally with the peasants and the urban poor and whose slogan was, 'When Adam delved and Eve span, who was then the gentleman?' Ball took the side of the poor against the rich.

The 1381 Peasants' Revolt is but one example. There were the various Christian sects, now Churches in their own right, which fought on the side of Parliament in the 1640 English revolution. They were preaching the basic principles of Christianity, and found themselves in conflict with the authority of the established Church.

The struggle between the rich and the poor has consistently been reflected in the political struggles in England between Parliament and the monarchy. It was during the English Civil War that the Dissenters grew stronger, established their Churches and made dissent acceptable as part of our religious scene. It was, however, a bitter struggle. Christians have been on the right side of progressive struggles, as other Christians have been on the wrong side, supporting the

Establishment against the people. The fact is, of course, that in Britain the Anglican Church is part of the Establishment. That is why I believe the Church of England should be disestablished as it is in Wales and Scotland. I once had a debate on radio with Selwyn Gummer about disestablishment, and I am pleased to say that we who were against the Church being the state Church won hands down.

Whilst I believe that genuine Christianity is political, that politics are an essential part of Christian thinking and that it is absurd for Conservatives to say that the Church should not be involved in politics, I do, however, agree that the last thing we want is a theocratic state. Wherever such states have existed, whatever the religion, they have been a disaster. One only has to look at the situation in Iran to see what harm a theocratic state can do. Equally in history, Spain, with its Roman Catholic monarchist government during the time of the Christian Spanish Empire, was an intolerant, despotic society which oppressed the poor, especially the poor in their colonies.

Equally in Geneva, the Calvinists were dictatorial, intolerant, and persecuted those who did not accept their views.

That, in my view, is not in line with God's concept as expressed by Christ. There must be tolerance and an acceptance of other people's views.

That is what Christ taught and that is why Christianity and Democratic Socialism are in line with each other.

Chapter 4

Life's Mystery and God's Existence

The honour of man and the honour of God are found only in the heart and the spirit of man, not in cosmos.
Roger Garaudy, from *Science and Faith in Teilhard de Chardin*

Earlier, I referred to the mystery of life. Why are we here on earth, and what is life's purpose? It is the question that has continuously exercised the minds of philosophers, theologians, scientists and others since mankind first began to concern itself with life's complexities. Philosophers, as we are aware, divide basically into two schools: the idealist and the materialist. Idealists accept the concept of God, a supreme being, because they believe the idea came first, while materialists reject religions and a belief in God, a supreme being, because God cannot be shown to have a material existence. There have, of course, been many shades of thinking amongst the two basic philosophies, and despite all the millions of words written and spoken about whether God exists or not, there has never been a definitive answer. Nor, in my view, can there be. It comes down to a matter of faith. That is why so many people say they are agnostic; they do not know, and are not going to worry about it one way or the other.

Why are we here?

Many such people become very self-centred, thinking only of themselves and their own lives. But there are others who do get involved in society, in the community, and do worry about what happens to their fellow human beings, to life as a whole, and are concerned about the future of the earth.

I have no real answer to the 64,000-dollar question: Why are we here? Could I answer that, the mystery of life would cease to be a mystery. What I always keep in mind, however, are the words of Nikolai Ostrovsky: 'Man's dearest possession is life. It is given to him but once, and he must live it so as to feel no torturing regrets for wasted years, never know the burning shame of a mean and petty past; so live that, dying, he might say: all my life, all my strength were given to the finest cause in all the world – the fight for the Liberation of Mankind.' I find that a wonderful statement and if one lives by it, one has truly lived a Christian life.

What sort of life should we try to live? I have said earlier that it is my view, which I believe to be the Christian view, that we should not sit in judgement on others. We must be understanding and compassionate. There is good and bad in us all. There are, of course, conflicting attitudes amongst Christians as to one's attitude to salvation. There are those who argue that pleasure and enjoyment are bad and must be avoided.

Some go to extremes, believing they must inflict pain on themselves in order to receive God's favour. That is in contrast to the Calvinists who accept the doctrine of predestination, a doctrine which argues that salvation does not depend upon one's own actions.

What one is clearly talking about here is one's moral conduct. In doing so, we should always remember what Christ said to those who were about to stone a woman for adultery. 'Let him who is without sin, cast the first stone' (John 8:7). Certainly, one should do one's best to lead a moral life. Cheating, lying, stealing, fornicating, are not to be recommended; but there can be circumstances when in order to uphold a moral position, one may be forced to do all kinds of things. If, for instance, to save someone from death or injury, one had to lie, then who could say one should not? If one's children were starving and the only way to save them was to steal from those with plenty, who can say that those in such dire need should not steal? One has only to examine the circumstances of a situation to recognise that answers cannot be glibly given to moral or any other questions, without acknowledging the complexity of the situation.

The world is a complex place. That is why it is mysterious, and many conflicting answers have been given regarding the complexity of life and death. For example, there are many ideas of what heaven is, and what it could be like. The Muslim idea of heaven is certainly different from the Christian idea. There are those who believe, not in heaven but in reincarnation and that we will come back at some time and live again, either once or many times. There are some who believe the reincarnation could be in other forms than as a human being. It is clear to me that many people fear death because they do not know what is going to happen to them. Are they going to heaven? Will they end up in hell? Will they be reincarnated? Or what? It is understandable that people should have such fears; but I believe that whether or not they are Christian, they should try to get rid of such fears. Death is not to be feared; it is life that can and often does hold horror for people.

The Christianity I accept is really about life here on earth, doing one's best to improve and change society, and making happiness and decency a reality here and now. I well remember the saying of Wittgenstein which explains that, 'death is not an event of life: we do not live to experience death'. There are people who consider it a grievance that they will ultimately be deprived of life. That is not a view I take.

There is evil in the world, and where it is obviously raising its ugly head it has to be combatted, but equally it has to be understood. War is evil and has to be combatted. Peace and justice are Christian concepts and they have to be striven for. Poverty is an evil, especially when at the same time extreme riches are flaunted, making the lot of the poor even harder to bear. Not to have a roof over one's head, to be forced to sleep rough in a cardboard box, is evil, and it must be a Christian priority to end such things. For people to be poorly clothed, cold and hungry is an evil and Christians should play their full part in ending a system which leads to such things.

Pushing drugs for money, putting greed before people is an evil, as is putting profit before the needs of all. The very system of greedy capitalism is an evil. In the years of Margaret Thatcher, the USA was looked upon as an example to emulate. I would not deny that the USA has some good things. But it is not the type of society a Christian should work for, even though it has a large Christian community.

George Lansbury

One of the great leaders of the Labour Party who was a Christian, was George Lansbury, who founded and built up the *Daily Herald*. In his day it was a great Labour paper. Lansbury put a Christian stamp on the *Daily Herald*. He said, 'As I was the editor we found it very easy to make our stand against all war a very definite one on Christian lines. My correspondence during the war [1914–1918] years and since convince me that much more than my Church or clergy, the *Herald* helped people to preserve their faith in religion.'

In 1918, he published an article entitled 'Christ's Call to Peace', which received a great response. The book which more than any other of Lansbury's advocated his Christian concepts was *Your Part in Poverty*. In it, George Lansbury argued that if Christianity was applied properly on earth, it would lead to a Socialist society.

The Christian, George Lansbury, went to prison as a councillor for what became known as 'Poplarism'. The councillors refused to cut unemployment benefits, etc., and insisted on building houses for the poor. What happened in Poplar had its reflection in Liverpool in 1984/5/6, but the difference was that in Lansbury's days the councillors were imprisoned and became martyrs, whereas in Liverpool they were surcharged and disqualified and made to appear irresponsible. What should be realised, however, is that the leader of the Liverpool Council was John Hamilton, a Quaker and very much a George Lansbury figure.

In his book *My Life*, George Lansbury wrote:

Whatever future there may be for me, my most cherished memories will be of the long, long years of work and pleasure, agitation and propaganda, carried on in the company with those countless numbers of people, most of whom possess no money, no property, but who do possess the greatest of God's gifts to men, the spirit of comradeship and loyalty to each other.

George Lansbury left his imprint on the Labour movement in Britain, and did so particularly because he was a Christian, who fought strong and hard to create God's Kingdom here on earth.

How does the life of Lansbury fit in with the mystery of life? It does so in the sense that one can never know what role one is going to play, yet when a good person comes along, he or she is recognised by those around him or her and no matter what happens they, as good people, leave their mark and are an inspiration to all those who knew them. Lansbury was a pacifist and suffered a great deal at the hands of people like Ernest Bevin. They tried to humiliate him, yet through his ordeal he remained gentle, humble and kind and will long be remembered in the Socialist movement when others are long forgotten.

Chance and design

Let me now try to answer the most serious question of all: Why are we here? Rationalist philosophers like A. J. Ayer argue that there is no design, there is no creator and that the argument for this is vacuous. He says that for there to be any substance in such an argument it would be necessary to specify the end for which the world was designed.

The design argument arose because it was pointed out that animals and humans had similar faculties, such as sight and hearing. There is also the pollination of flowers, the dependence of parasites upon other forms of life. David Hume, in his *Dialogues Concerning Natu-*

ral Religion, argued that such ideas did not apply to the world as a whole.

It has been argued, in my opinion, rightly, that 'it cannot all just be a fluke.' That is what I believe. I am not competent enough to know all the answers. I am not a philosopher; but precisely because the world is so complex, there must be more than just what we see. I realise that daily the mysteries of life are being cleared up, but as one mystery is understood another one appears. I understand this more than I ever did.

About nine months ago, while in hospital after an operation, I was informed that I had a fatal disease and that little could be done for me – it was only a matter of time. It was a traumatic experience but the truth is that, despite all the medical science and treatment available, the mystery of life remains. I have no answer to that mystery, but it is real enough.

All of us are but specks of dust on the earth's surface. Although we shall depart this world, enter heaven and our bodies return to dust, life and the world continue. It is that which is also positive; but in today's world there is also danger, because unless action is taken to end wars, with their frightful weapons, and at the same time to deal with the ecological problems, man will destroy the earth and all that lives on it.

The real point is that God gave us all free will. Clearly, we can either use that free will for good, or we can be stupid and destroy ourselves. Since my illness, it has been said to me, 'I suppose you are angry and feel, why me?' I said to the consultant who put this to me, 'Why not me?' It has happened to thousands of people, why should I be special?

Naturally, one's mind becomes focused when one has to face such a situation. I have certainly given the mystery of life a great deal of thought, and gone over my life, and I have come to very much the same conclusion that Philip Toynbee came to, expressed in his autobiographical journal *End of a Journey*, when he was faced with a similar situation. He said, 'I am distressed at the thought of not seeing those I love any more, or being seen by them. But otherwise there are no old experiences which I long to repeat, and no new ones which I long to try.'

Philip Toynbee was for most of his life an unbeliever, but converted to Roman Catholicism in his later years. Converts, as we are all aware, can be greater proselytisers than those born into their religion.

I am certainly not a convert. I was born an Anglican and after 1968 went back to my Church. I saw no reason to convert to Roman Catholicism or to any other section of Christianity. In any case, the Church should be universal, covering a wide spectrum from extreme orthodoxy to the latest modern trend. Yet, and it's a big yet, the Church must carry out God's work, based on the teachings of Christ – the revolutionary, reformist carpenter – the son of working people. That is the true meaning and essence of Christian love. As Philip Toynbee says, 'There have been more martyrs to the Christianity of Hate and the Christianity of Self-Righteousness than there have been to the Christianity of Love.'

It is the Christianity of love that I want to see prevail, the Christianity of understanding, of compassion, of the unity of all, the Christianity that will build the new society. That is what I believe God wants us to do.

Chapter 5

Conservative Christianity

A smooth and easy life, an uninterrupted enjoyment of the goods of providence, full meals, soft raiment, well furnished homes, the pleasures of sense, the feeling of security, the consciousness of wealth – these and the like, if we are not careful, choke up all the avenues of the soul through which the light and breath of heaven might come to us.

John Henry Newman, *Parochial and Plain Sermons*

One can be a Christian whatever one's political outlook. That cannot possibly be denied, although I personally find it difficult to equate right-wing Conservative or Fascist ideas with the teachings of Christ. With regard to the Conservatives, most of those who are Christian take the view that the Church ought not to meddle in politics and should instead concentrate on saving individual souls. It should not become involved in collective earthly salvation.

The position of the right-wing radical Conservatives was clearly expounded in Margaret Thatcher's speech to the Assembly of the Church of Scotland in 1988. The emphasis was placed on individual responsibility. 'What is certain, however, is that any set of social and economic arrangements which is not founded on the acceptance of individual responsibility will do nothing but harm. We are all responsible for our own actions. We cannot blame society if we disobey the law.'

There is a great deal of truth in this – but what about collective responsibility? Are we not our brothers' and our sisters' keepers? In her speech, Mrs Thatcher quoted St Paul's second letter to the Thessalonians: 'If a man will not work, he shall not eat' (3:10). She then went on to say, 'Abundance rather than poverty has a legitimacy which derives from the very nature of creation.' I have carefully studied her arguments, but for me, she misses the whole point. Workers do work hard, by their efforts they do create the wealth in society; and then too often the fruits of their labour are taken from them. On the other hand, too many owners or shareholders do not work, yet reap the rewards. What St Paul was concerned about were the rich who did not work. He wanted a redistribution of wealth. It is that redistribution of wealth, created by the workers, that the Conservatives resist. They are not in favour of higher taxes on the rich and want to reduce them, thus giving them even more riches at the expense of the poor. The Conservatives, in fact, turn Christianity on its head.

Tory theology

In the book, *Christianity and Conservatism*, the best argued case for Conservatism is made by Lord Griffiths, in a chapter headed, 'The Conservative Quadrilateral'. He takes issue with an address given by the Bishop of Durham in 1986 on 'The Market' in which, he says, 'In essence, what the Bishop and others have done is to define modern Conservatism as materialistic, secular and individualistic, and that seems to be the very antithesis of the Gospel. Therefore they have no option but to reject it.'

Griffiths says that the Bishop has misunderstood what the Conservatives are doing, and that 'in a theological context . . . it rests firmly within the Judaeo-Christian tradition. It follows that the Churches should respect modern Conservatism as a legitimate political option for Christians.'

To Griffiths, 'The engine driving prosperity and employment in the last decade has been the growth of small firms and self-employment. And in almost all cases the success of small firms is associated with the leadership of one or at most a few individuals. This emphasis on the individual was also the basis for recent trade union reforms in Britain.' There are several points to make about his formulation.

It is true that, in the Thatcher years, there was a growth in small firms, but that was because in the main the great centres of manufacturing industry were allowed to go to the wall, and those who suffered, as could be expected, endeavoured to find a way out of their problems by creating small firms. The truth is they were not all successful; thousands have closed down, and the savings which those involved put into them have been lost. With regard to self-employment, that is not necessarily a good thing. In the construction industry, for example, it can and does lead to chaos, poor workmanship, disregard of safety regulations, and can be very detrimental to the workforce.

The claim that the trade unions have been handed back to the individual member is sheer mythology. The legislation was designed to weaken the power of the unions, and in doing so, that weakens the strength of the individual trade unionist.

The legislation was not pro-individual, it was anti-union, and designed to help the employer – capital against labour. Experience has shown that employment conditions and wages can only seriously be negotiated collectively. It is impossible to get decent conditions through individual bargaining, particularly when unemployment is high, as it was throughout the Thatcher years. As the Church of England's *Faith in the City* report says, 'We believe that at present too much emphasis is being given to individualism and not enough to collective obligation.' Griffiths quotes these words disparagingly. He tries to defend the Conservative view by saying that 'defending the individual is very different from defending individualism', which, he agrees, 'is at root a deeply non-Christian, if not anti-Christian, philosophy.' He argues that Conservative government policies are not individualist in that sense. All I can say is, you could have fooled me!

Griffiths tries to have it both ways. He accepts that 'our Lord, in the New Testament sums up the laws of the Old Testament as just two precepts: love of God and love of neighbour. Therefore, Cain's question, "Am I my brother's keeper?" is answered directly by our Lord's words, "Love your neighbour as yourself".'

But then he goes on to say, 'What, however, modern Conservatism refuses to do is to equate this necessary concern for others with the pursuit of equality or corporatism. All too often in the eyes of the Church in recent years the litmus test of compassion has been whether egalitarian policies are being advanced.'

That, in essence, sums up the position. There is no doubt that Griffiths argues a case which, although liberally using various Church sources and dignitaries, is, in reality, the opposite of what Christianity stands for. It is cleverly done, but in the last analysis I believe it is the opposite of what Christ and his disciples believed. For example, he says, 'Christian theology reminds us of our obligations to our neighbours, but it offers no justification for compelling others to submit to the pursuit of economic equality by governments.'

Again, there is some truth in this, but if one accepts that 'I am my brother's keeper', then surely those in power must work to create a society that brings about equality, and fairness based on equality.

Choice and equality

It is amazing how the words of Archbishop William Temple, in his book, *Christianity and Social Order*, are used by Griffiths to try to justify the Conservative policy on choice. I can't help feeling that Temple's words have been distorted. For example, he is quoted as saying, 'If each man and woman is a child of God, whom God loves and for whom Christ died, then there is in each a worth absolutely independent of all usefulness to society. The person is primary, not the society; the State exists for the citizen, not the citizen for the State. The first aim of the social progress must be to give the fullest possible scope for the exercise of all powers and qualities which are distinctly personal, and of these the most fundamental to deliberate choice.'

Griffiths then further quotes the Archbishop: 'It is the responsible exercise of deliberate choice which most fully expresses personality and best deserves the great name of freedom.'

No one can seriously disagree with William Temple. But what Griffiths does is to gloss over the Archbishop's words, 'The State exists for the citizen, not the citizen for the State'. That is really the key. The Archbishop wrote his book in 1942, at the height of the war. It should be remembered that we were in conflict with the German Nazi regime, where the citizens were subordinated to the state and where the citizens were expected to exist for the state. There was no choice for the individual. Perhaps Brian Griffiths has not seen the letter which appeared in *The Times* on 21st December 1940, signed by the Archbishops of Canterbury and

York, the Cardinal Archbishop of Westminster and the Moderator of the Free Churches.

The letter set out five principles upon which they felt a lasting peace could be established:

1. Extreme inequality in wealth and possessions should be abolished.
2. Every child, regardless of race or class, should have equal opportunities of education, suitable for the development of his peculiar capabilities.
3. The family as a social unit must be safeguarded.
4. The sense of a Divine vocation must be restored to man's daily work.
5. The resources of the earth should be used as God's gifts to the whole human race, and used with due consideration for the needs of the present and future generations.

The Archbishop of York went further. On 7th January 1941, in a speech at a conference in Malvern, he said:

> . . . the Church can point to those features of our existing society which, while they can never prevent individual men and women from becoming Christians, are contrary to divine justice, and act as stumbling blocks, making it harder for men to live Christian lives. In our present situation we believe that the maintenance of that part of the structure of our society by which the ultimate ownership of the principal industrial resources of the community can be vested in the hands of private owners, may be such a stumbling block.

He went on to say, 'The time has come for Christians to proclaim the need for striving towards a form of society in which, while the essential value of the individual human personality is preserved, the continuance of those values will be no longer possible.' He further said, 'To a large extent production is carried on not to supply the consumer with goods, but to bring profits to the producer, and the producer in turn is often subordinated to the purely financial ends of those who own the capital plant or supply the credit to erect or work it.'

At the time, the Archbishop of York was Dr William Temple. I could give further chapter and verse of what William Temple thought, said and wrote. It is amazing how Brian Griffiths can use Temple's words to argue a case which in essence was the very opposite of what Temple believed. At all times he rightly stressed the importance of the individual, of individual freedom, but he accepted that collective responsibility and action was the best way to preserve and develop such personal freedom.

The example of housing

Lord Griffiths makes much of council house sales, saying that this 'choice' means that families can gain independence and provide for their children. It is a totally false argument. Each council house sold, took away the hopes of those who could not buy, so that today we have a housing crisis for the poorer sections of society of gigantic proportions. Why, after selling council houses, were the councils not allowed to use the money saved, to build more council houses to meet the needs of those who could not afford to buy? Why are councils not allowed to build houses for sale as well as for rent? It was sheer political dogma which stopped the councils from doing such things. The real choice was limited, and is the opposite of caring and concern for the have-nots in society.

To argue his case, Griffiths is forced to quote what Christ actually said, and what the Bible says, 'Woe to you that are rich . . .' 'How hard it is for those who have riches to enter the Kingdom of God' . . . 'You cannot serve God and mammon.' Griffiths says that the Bishop of Durham's view is a caricature of modern Conservatism, and that 'any serious discussion of wealth creation must confront the need for individual choice and the freedom of markets.'

Does he not realise that millions of our citizens have no individual choice? They are forced, because of circumstances, to take what they can get. They have no jobs, they have no home of their own. They may have the minimum of clothes, they cannot afford to eat in restaurants, they cannot choose where their children go to school. Choice is a myth, and despite all that has been said about this Conservative government, the situation for thousands of our people has got worse, not better. Some have gained from the Thatcher society, but today even they are realising that Thatcherism has been a myth.

The chapter in *Christianity and Conservatism* which really answers the Conservative case on the poor is that by Frank Field, 'How Well Have Britain's Poor Fared?' in which he says, 'The Government is hard-pressed to demonstrate that the trickle-down theory is about to work, let alone that it has worked over the past decade.'

Frank Field points out that those in the poorest groups have experienced living standards well below those groups on average incomes. The data outlined in his chapter give the lie to the Conservative claims that in the last eleven years the poor benefited under Mrs Thatcher.

The assertion that the Conservatives have carried out the teachings of the Gospel has, in my opinion, been proved to be incorrect. It is a smokescreen which serves to hide the reality of how the poor, the unfortunate, the dispossessed, have suffered, and are still suffering. These are the reasons why I feel that the word of God as expressed through Christ has no real place in Conservative official politics. The Church leaders have been right to point out this fact.

Chapter 6

Why Disestablishment is Necessary

> Thomas More simply said that he died in and for the faith of the Holy Catholic Church 'as the King's good servant, but God's first'.
>
> E. E. Reynolds, *Saint Thomas More*

Should the Church of England continue to be the Established Church, the 'National Church', called such by Samuel Taylor Coleridge? It is a question which will, I believe, be debated increasingly in years to come. As we all know, it became the Church of England during the reign of Henry VIII who had been designated 'Defender of the Faith' by the Pope. To this day, English monarchs bear the title. The faith Henry was defending was the Catholic faith. He was no Protestant. His argument with the Pope was not about doctrine but about the future of the monarchy. He wanted a divorce, which the Church refused to grant him; this, despite the fact that

Henry had written strongly against the Protestant heretics and to that extent his outlook was similar to that of Thomas More and Erasmus.

The historical backdrop

The struggle between Henry and the Church was fought out with Thomas More being a prominent player. More was a complex character. He wrote *Utopia*, a type of socialist-orientated tract, but at the same time he was orthodox and fought hard against heresy. He clearly, but wrongly, believed, as a devout Christian, that sexuality was a slide into hell. After he had completed his legal studies he gave a series of lectures at the Church of St Lawrence Jewry. More's lectures were based on his reading and study of *The City of God* by Augustine of Hippo, who believed that all sensuality was evil, and bitterly criticised Julian of Eclanum, saying, 'What sober minded man would not prefer to take food, dry or moist, without any stinging carnal pleasure, if he could, as the air draws in and lets out into the surrounding air by inhaling and exhaling?'

There is no doubt that Thomas More's views on sensuality, despite his later marriage which produced three children, were important during the arguments between Henry VIII and the Roman Church. He wrote *A Dialogue Concerning Heresies* in which he attacked Martin Luther and his ideas. As far as More was concerned, Luther's worst sins, apart from his heresies, were his teachings about marriage as well as the doctrine of predestination.

Henry VIII based his case for a divorce on the book of Leviticus. Because of that, he wanted the Bible translated into English and made available to the people, so that they would understand his case.

That period in England was one of great upheaval.

Heresy was on the increase and a lawyer named Simon Fish fiercely attacked the clergy. In 1528, he published a tract against them, *A Supplication for the Beggars*. To some extent it surprisingly showed the influence of More's *Utopia*. What Fish did was to make an appeal on behalf of the beggars which, he said, infested England. He argued that there were beggars because the clergy took so much money and there was not enough left to pay people to work.

At the time that Fish issued his pamphlet, Thomas More was Lord Chancellor. Henry VIII made contact with Fish as he felt Fish could be of use to him. He advised More not to take action against Fish, at which Thomas More promptly arrested Fish's wife. Although More's *Utopia* is considered by Karl Kautsky, for instance, as one of the first Socialist tracts, More nevertheless believed that anti-clericalism, heresy and sedition always went hand in hand.

Henry increasingly came into conflict with the Church over his demand for a divorce. The Pope refused to agree to this and as a result Henry became more and more antagonistic towards him. By August 1530, Henry was saying that England had never really been subject to the Papacy and began to spread the word that unless the Pope agreed he would withdraw from the Roman Communion. It was recognised that if that took place, he would be taking the Church of England out of Roman Catholic control. Thomas More was not in agreement with that and said so.

Space prevents me from giving the full details of Henry's campaign against the clergy. He bullied the Convocation, by threats, blackmail and other questionable tactics, to make him the Supreme Head of the Church in England.

More reacted by saying he would resign his position as Lord Chancellor as soon as possible. Step by step Henry took the Church in England out of the Roman domain. Eventually, More was arrested and finally executed. Henry had won. The Church in England became independent of the Roman Church, and although it continued to be Catholic in dogma, stage by stage it became influenced by Protestantism until, through the Thirty-Nine Articles, a compromise was reached. That is why the Church of England has both a Catholic and a Protestant basis, and in this respect is unique in the world. The Church became an instrument of the state and the Church of England the state religion.

At various stages, Catholics were persecuted, as were the Protestant dissenters. The struggle for religious freedom over the centuries has been long and bitter.

Samuel Taylor Coleridge

In 1830, Samuel Taylor Coleridge wrote a book, *On the Constitution of the Church and the State*. Coleridge was an ardent supporter of the French revolution when a student, and with Robert Southey created an organisation to establish new progressive societies in America. As the years passed he moved to a Conservative position and in the end became a real Tory. He did, however, argue that Roman Catholics should be in the House of Commons.

In his book, Coleridge wrote:

> The fourth character of the Christian Church and a necessary consequence of the first and third, is its Catholicity, i.e. universality. It is neither Anglican, Gallican nor Roman, neither Latin nor Greek. Even the Catholic and Apostolic Church of England is a less safe expression than the Churches of Christ in England: though the Catholic Church *in*, or (what would be still better,) the Catholic Church under Christ throughout Great Britain and Ire-

land, is justifiable and appropriate: for through the presence of its only head and sovereign, entire in each and one in all, the Church universal is spiritually perfect in every true Church, and of course in any number of such Churches, which from circumstance of place, or the community of country or of language, we have occasion to speak of collectively.

Coleridge makes a clear distinction between the national Church and the Christian Church.

I have quoted Coleridge at such length because he describes the position of the Church of England in relation to the Christian Church as a whole. It is unique because of the actions of Henry leading to the breakaway from the Roman Church, yet at the same time accepting the catholicity of the Church, its universality.

It is possible, though doubtful, that there could have been a justifiable argument in the past for the Church being national. The link between Church and state today, however, is in my view totally unjustified. One hears, of course, warnings that if the Church were to be disestablished then a great constitutional crisis would ensue and the position of the monarch would be put at risk. The bishops are certainly divided on the issue, although the majority are firmly opposed to disestablishment.

Years ago I read a brilliant article calling for disestablishment, by Bishop Trevor Huddleston. I was so taken with it I invited the Bishop to lunch with me to discuss the question, after which I was even more convinced that the case he presented was correct. Up to then I had not taken a firm line on the issue, but from that point on I felt it my duty, in the interests of the Church and the people, to support the disestablishment of the Church of England.

The situation today

In the House of Commons, Church legislation still goes before the House, is debated and voted upon. It is true that, since the General Synod was strengthened, the Church itself has a greater say than in the past, yet legislation still appears for agreement and confirmation because that is the constitution. At that stage, every MP can take part in the debate and vote, irrespective of whether they are Christians, atheists, Muslims, Jews, Roman Catholics or Protestant dissenters. It is a ridiculous situation and should be ended. The affairs of the Church should be confined to the Church, and at no time should the issues concerning the Church of England be brought before Parliament.

What makes it even more galling is that Welsh MPs can speak and vote on these questions, yet the Church in Wales is disestablished. The Scots can speak and vote on Church of England issues, yet they have their own national Church of Scotland, also headed by the monarch.

The quicker the Church is disestablished, therefore, the better for everyone, and the better for Christianity. The concept of creating God's Kingdom on earth does not entail a state Church which could act against other Churches, leading to uniformity of worship and belief.

We have had that in England in the past, backed up by Church taxes such as the tithes which, over the years, caused much conflict between the Church and state on the one hand and the people on the other. I am convinced that the tie-up of the Church of England with the state is a hindrance to Christian development. That is why the link must be broken. The fact that it has been a state Church since the time of Henry VIII is not a case for its continuation, and is not a good enough reason for the link not to be broken.

As I have said elsewhere, intolerance, and the imposition of a state religion, are not in line with Christian teaching, and clearly the time has come when state and Church should be separated once and for all. It has been said that, should that happen, the size of Church congregations will decline; that there will be less interest in the Church, because to be a Christian will entail a conscious effort instead of being more or less automatically assumed as it is now.

Church schools

This raises the whole question as to whether Christianity should be compulsorily taught in schools. Should there be Church schools of any denomination? I believe that religion should be taught, but it ought to be comparative religion, including the rationalist arguments. With regard to Church schools, I believe they should be phased out. We already have Church of England schools, Roman Catholic schools, and now the demand is growing for Muslim schools. Some of my friends on the left of the Labour Party are advocating this because they feel it wrong to discriminate against any section of the community. That is a powerful argument, but the answer is not to extend various religious schools but to have comparative religion taught in all our schools.

With regard to the provision of religious instruction, that can be arranged outside the national educational system. The Churches, and the various religious organisations, can provide that themselves. The important thing is to create universality, true catholicism, and that can be developed through the state educational system, including the voluntary part of that system, which should become an integral part of it.

'Why,' my journalist friend may say, 'concentrate so much on the Church of England, and the issue of state and Church?' The answer is really simple. Because we live in England, because the Church is a state Church and because it affects our attitude towards Christianity – unfortunately, it cannot be ignored. It can and does affect one's attitude to God. If God is seen to be the instrument of the state, and the powers that be use the state religion to strengthen a particular type of political system, that can and does cause people to reject Christianity, considering it to be the instrument of the political enemy.

The Church of England was described in the past as the Tory Party at prayer. That is no longer quite as true as it was, although some Tory MPs would like it to be, and continue by their actions and speeches to claim the Church as if it were theirs exclusively. That, I believe is the best reason for disestablishment. The Church should be free of the state, and standing on its own two feet it can then be the rallying force for all the people to build a better, just and Christian society.

Chapter 7

Christians who have Influenced my Life

He who attempts to set up God's Kingdom in his heart, furthers it in the world.

Cardinal John Henry Newman,
Parochial and Plain Sermons

There is no doubt that one's life is affected and influenced by those one meets and gets to know. In the course of a relatively long life one meets and mixes with a very wide cross section of people. The one thing I have learned is that, irrespective of race, colour, class, religion or other such traits, men and women are made in the image of God and are, therefore, central to Christianity.

I have met and mixed with 'saints' as well as 'sinners', some who are decent, fair and compassionate and others who are the very opposite. The interesting thing is that some people are a combination of good and bad.

Some have clearly influenced me more than others,

not necessarily because of their intellectual prowess, or because they were smart or clever, but because of the way in which they conducted their lives. In their own way they were 'saints' just as much as St Francis of Assisi was; and to me, he was the greatest of all the saints.

John Wheatley

In March 1989, I gave one of a series of Lenten Lectures called *Mirrors of God* at St Margaret's Church, the parish church for the Houses of Parliament (see Appendix I). I had been invited to talk about my ideas on what constituted a saint, and to give an example.

I thought long and hard about this and a number of people came to mind, but because I was an MP, and because St Margaret's is the MPs' church, I chose to lecture on John Wheatley, the Labour Roman Catholic MP, who was Minister of Health in the 1924 Labour government, and who at the time was responsible for housing. In my view, Wheatley was a saintly figure. I take the view that if it is accepted that a saint is close to God and accessible to man, then John Wheatley had both those attributes. He was close to God and accessible to man. He was doing God's work here on earth. What he did for housing for the poor was outstanding. He was spurred on by his own experiences of living in slum housing when a child. The Wheatley Act of 1924 set council housing on its way. He believed passionately that everyone had a right to a decent home in which to live.

Wheatley was a Christian, and like Keir Hardie, George Lansbury and Stafford Cripps, related his Christianity to his work as a Labour MP. It was Wheatley who in Scotland created the Catholic Socialist Society, at first in opposition to the hierarchy, but in the end they accepted it, some giving it support. He led a Christian life which he dedicated to the poor.

Uncle Dom

One of the people I thought about who, like Wheatley, was doing God's work and on whom I considered basing my lecture, was someone in a much more humble position, living in a council house, but who was one of the finest men I ever met. I am referring to my wife's uncle, Dominic Barrett. Uncle Dom, as we called him, was simple, humble, quiet and led a truly Christian life, a shining example to all who came into contact with him.

He was by no means a 'goody-goody'. He never criticised others. He understood the waywardness of people and always showed great compassion. He really did understand the teachings of his Creator and to the best of his ability followed them.

My wife and I lived for some months with Uncle Dom, his wife Auntie Ruth, and their daughter Monica. When we went to Liverpool in 1947, we had nowhere to live at first and so he let us stay with him and his family in Huyton. It should be remembered I was then a Communist and atheist and Uncle Dom was neither. Not once did he ever show any hostility to me for my views.

He was a man who devoted himself to others. At work, in Crawfords' biscuit factory, he was a trade union representative, a strong trade unionist who supported the Labour Party and staunchly defended the rights of workers at his place of work. He was also a welfare/sick visitor for the Catholic Church, visiting those who were ill or destitute and making sure they were properly looked after. He never made a song and dance about his work for the St Vincent de Paul Society but carried it out efficiently and with great compassion. I admired him enormously, and there is no doubt that his main strength was his Christianity.

He believed and he put his beliefs into practice. During the whole time we lived at his home, and shared his table and his life, I never heard him use a cross word against his wife and daughter, although Monica could be trying in the mornings when she would not get up early enough to get off to work on time!

He and Auntie Ruth, devout Roman Catholics, were not bigots. Monica, in fact, married a Protestant with their blessing. Uncle Dom also had his wife's sister and family living in his house for some time during the war. Aunt Miriam, like my mother-in-law, was a Methodist, not a Catholic, yet they were made welcome and not a word of disagreement passed between them. In fact, Aunt Miriam was also a good Christian woman, warm-hearted, helpful and the sort that would do anything to help others. She was part of the Conley family, who were all good-living people, one of the finest being my mother-in-law. Nothing was ever too much for her. I have naturally been much influenced by such a good Christian family. It would have been impossible not to have found some of their goodness rubbing off on me. Honesty and decency were part of their make-up, and clearly stemmed from their Christian views.

These experiences in life cannot be overlooked. People's outlook, religion and ideas have to be taken into consideration when appraising them. Often in Liverpool they say about someone, 'She is a good Christian woman,' or 'He is a good Christian man.' That says it all. It means they are generous, not mean-spirited, will help others and have understanding and compassion. They make allowances and do not easily judge others, but accept the biblical statement, 'Do unto others as you would have them do unto you.'

Am I being indulgent? Perhaps I am, but I write as I feel and that is how I feel about the people I have lived with and represented for so long.

The good and the godly

I have found too, in the wider public, in the Labour Party and trade unions, many, many people who have led good lives, constantly giving without expecting or wanting anything in return – people, for instance, like Joe O'Grady, who for years, every month came to my interviews with constituents, giving hours of service for nothing, just in order to help his fellow constituents, and in the process helping me as the MP. I can think of the youngsters, now not so young, in Warbreck Ward, who set up a group to do housework, painting and decorating and much else for elderly people. Most of the group were Catholic, but not all, and their assistance was not confined to Catholic families. The same youngsters were politically active in CND, and many were in the Labour Party.

I can think of Frank Reeves and Dave Lloyd in Fazakerley, Catholic and Protestant respectively, who in their spare time helped the aged, the sick and the deprived. There are many, many more like these, too numerous to record. These are all people who accept responsibility, not just for themselves but for others, for society, and they do this because they believe and accept Christ's teaching.

I admit that I have been profoundly affected by such people and often in their presence have felt very humble. They do good things, not because they are priests, ministers or dignitaries of their Churches, but because they believe it to be right. I can hear people saying that there are people who help others who are not Christians, who are unbelievers. I accept that, but whether they know it or not, they too are doing God's work.

It will be said, 'But this is charity, it is voluntary and in line with Conservative thinking.' Yes, it is voluntary. Yes, there is some charity involved. What is interesting, however, is that the same people doing these things are the very ones who believe that support should be given by the state as a right, and not through charity alone. That is the difference between the true Christian attitude and the view that the poor and needy should be helped by charity. The old saying, 'as cold as charity', arises from the attitude that people should be grateful for charity, when in fact they ought to be receiving the necessary assistance by right, without strings attached.

I have, of course, met people who were not Christians who played their part in helping those in need. It would be absurd to say that the 'saints' were all Christians. But I have to be honest and say that my experience has been that Christians of various denominations have been well to the fore in such work, and this has affected my outlook.

If people have a basically Christian attitude to life and live according to Christian principles, then clearly, if they have led good lives, it must have had something to do with their beliefs.

I have personally been more influenced in my private life by lay Christians than by priests or ministers. Yet some priests and ministers have influenced me. There is Father Fitzgerald of Walton, now a Parish Priest in Leigh, Lancashire who preached the social gospel and openly took the side of the poor, as did Alan Taylor, one of the Anglican priests of Walton parish church. Alan is now in Leeds, with a parish of his own. For a time he went to Mirfield and was a novice for the Community of the Resurrection. After a period he decided not to become a member of the Order but still remained firm in his Catholic views within the Church.

I am not saying that those I have mentioned were responsible for my going back to the Church, but they certainly helped me to realise that in the Church there were Christians whose lifestyle and goodness were worth emulating.

Chapter 8

Democracy in the Church

The Church's first task is to denounce the unjust structures not as one who judges from without, but as one who acknowledges his own share of the responsibility and the blame.

Archbishop Helder Camara,
Touching Ground, Taking Root

My Christianity is by no means orthodox, although I believe it to be traditional, based upon the early teachings of the Church, particularly the Gospels and the New Testament. I admit I cannot accept every statement in the New Testament. Apart from the obscurity of some of them, they can also be contradictory. What I am convinced about, however, is that there must be greater democracy in the Church. This is a demand that arose at the early stages of the Church, particularly after Constantine agreed to Christianity being the state religion of the Roman Empire. Prior to Constantine, the Church had not been totally hierarchical.

Hans Küng, in his *Why Priests?* pointed out, 'The history of ministries in the Church is unusually complex and varied. In the primitive period . . . local communities had different forms of organisations which only gradually . . . became conflated in the relatively useful system of a monarchical episcopate with presbyters and deacons.'

Back to the people

There has long been an argument about the nature of the Apostolic succession. The original disciples were regarded as individuals carrying out Christ's work. The laying on of hands, creating future apostles, (i.e., the bishops, etc.), was a development that took place once the Church became part of the state apparatus.

The early primitive Church gradually turned into its opposite. A large bureaucracy was created, and as the volume of written material increased, slowly but surely the early ideas and objectives of the Church were lost sight of. It is a fascinating story, which has parallels with what happened in the Soviet Union regarding Communist policy and organisation, once the Communist Party became the only legal political party in the Soviet Union.

Consistently, over the centuries, people inside the Church demanded a greater say, and forms of democratic organisation. That led to all types of 'heretics', from the Albigenses, the Hussites, the Lollards, to our present-day Liberation Theologians, whose concern is to set up organisations of the 'base', where priests need not be involved, yet the Mass is still performed and accepted.

In England and Scotland, Churches arose which set up democratic methods of Church structure. Lay people became members of committees and councils, and these became the power within the Church organisation.

In the Anglican Church, the trend towards greater democratic control of Church organisation has slowly gone forward. Over the years we have seen the General Synod become increasingly influential.

There are many in the Church who regret this. They are not enthusiastic about the role of the Synod and would like to return to the old system, where the real power was in the hands of the bishops.

Women's ordination

This is particularly true regarding the proposal for women priests in the Church of England and the wider Anglican Communion. There is a threat from some in the Church, mainly Anglo-Catholics, that they will split the Church if women become priests. Although I believe such a split would not be too damaging, it is nevertheless a genuine threat. It is not true to suggest, however, that all Anglo-Catholics take the view that there should not be women priests. In the event of women being ordained, most will remain within the Church and give them full and welcoming support.

In today's Church, women priests will eventually be accepted and although it might take longer, the Roman Catholic Church too will accept the principle and there will be women priests in the Roman Church.

There have been women ministers in some of the Protestant Churches for years. My brother-in-law, a Methodist, was married by a woman minister in the 1950s and those present at the service were not at all put out or surprised.

Eventually, that will be the case amongst the Anglicans and others who continue to follow the male Apostolic succession. The argument about women priests is part of the democratic process which, despite sturdy efforts by some to stop it, cannot be avoided.

In considering Christ's ideas, one must look at the impact they had on the so-called 'common man'. It is clear that, when the people first heard the gospel as preached by Christ, they were greatly affected. They clearly understood what he was saying. Christ both revealed and inspired. He not only showed the way mankind could and should go, he also inspired the individual to accept a life he or she could follow.

Looking back on the history of Christianity, it is amazing how simple the gospel seemed to the ordinary man and woman. Yet, as time has gone on, it has become more and more caught up in dogma and doctrines, in decisions of Ecumenical Councils, in philosophies, in Vatican Decrees, Anglican Articles, Calvinistic Institutions, in Athanasian, Nicene and Apostolic Creeds, and in all manner of issues which were discussed at length and disputed by the sophisticated.

The trouble is, the original simplicity of Christ's teaching has long disappeared in clouds of complicated dogma and too often mysterious ceremony. To the mass of ordinary people it seemed perfectly natural for them to conform in their lives to Christ's teachings.

Since the Second Vatican Council, the hierarchy of the Roman Church has made certain concessions concerning the involvement of the laity in Christian worship. The priesthood is no longer as remote as it was, yet it is still only a half-way house. The ideas of Leonardo Boff have been attacked, and Cardinal Ratzinger of the Vatican took steps against Boff and his works. The hierarchy retreated only after great pressure from the bishops from Boff's own country, who travelled to Rome in order to defend him.

There is no doubt that, despite its often tyrannical attitudes, the institutional Church has been a great civilising force in the world, especially in Europe. Yet it has been largely the so-called dissident Christians who have championed social freedom, freedom of thought as well as democracy, and have given us a deeper understanding of what can be called an integral religion.

Dean Inge once said that the Christian faith is 'a vital energy of the whole man'. Troeltsch wrote, 'At bottom things are extremely simple if we are willing to see them as they really are.'

To the so-called common man, Christ's teachings have been clear and simple, and have helped create the whole man. That is what we as Christians must strive to achieve – a simple explanation of Christ's teachings, so that a better world can be built, a world of love and not hate, a world of peace and not violence, a world of justice, not oppression.

God is part of each of us, and it is that belief that we must fully understand when we are working to create his Kingdom on earth

Back to the roots

Because the Church had strayed from the teachings of its early days, many wanted to form communities which would keep alive the early Christian spirit. Groups of men and women created religious orders and lived a communal life, a type of communistic life, owning all things in common, creating their monasteries and convents. It was in those institutions that the radicalism of the Christian ethics of the early days of the Church was pursued. The authorities of the Church were not too happy with these developments, but practical politics forced them to accept them and in the long run the religious orders were more or less brought within Church control. This happened even to the organisation created by St Francis. Father Bede Jarrett, in his *Social*

Theories of the Middle Ages, argues, 'The work of St Francis was . . . not so much the founding of an Order as an appeal of a lover of Christ to all men to go back to the Gospel of Christ. What St Francis wanted was a straighter and poorer life, a Christian communism.' The *Cambridge Mediaeval History* says of St Francis and his supporters , 'The Spiritual Party contained both lay and clerical elements, and had political, doctrinal and revolutionary, as well as pure mystical objectives.'

The official Church has been forced to adapt. When it has not done so splits have occurred, and so-called heretical movements have arisen which eventually led to the Reformation, splitting the Church from top to bottom.

All of this has been part of the struggle for greater democracy in the Church. It is, as I have said above, a struggle which continues to this day, and because of the nature of modern society, it will intensify.

The early Church

In his book *Why Priests?* Hans Küng puts forward an argument for greater democratic structures in the Church. One does not have to accept all he says, but it is clear that he is making a powerful plea for greater democracy and involvement of the laity. His programme has four basic proposals: (1) that there is a collegial responsibility of all members of the Church; (2) that there should be elections of Church leaders by the community in question; (3) that the public character of the Church requires a degree of clarity and openness of Church activities; and (4) that the relative independence of communities means there should be greater autonomy in respect of the universal Church.

Küng's proposals would be a fundamental break with past practice and I can understand why he was not received with enthusiasm by the hierarchy in the Church. Yet, whether one likes it or not, such ideas are more or less accepted in some Churches, and in time will have to be accepted by all the main Churches. The Church cannot live in isolation. It cannot divorce itself from the real world. If it does, it will only be a matter of time before it ceases to have any relevant function in society. The Church must adapt or die.

By adapting, the Church can again take on the ideas of the early Church and its basic Christian concepts. That is what it is doing in Latin America, and that is why a real living Church exists there. It is also the reason why it is hated so much by the rich and powerful, because the ideas of Christ lead to a questioning of society, and a demand for a better world, especially for the 'ordinary people'.

The struggle for democracy, for the involvement of the laity in Church life, for the ordination of women, are an essential part of the renewal of the Church. As old political concepts falter, it is clear that the struggle for a new world does not cease. The need to overcome oppression does not go away. The need for justice and peace continues, and it is through the Church, with its Liberation Theology, that a new way forward is demonstrated. It is possible that the best of Marxism (the real Marxism, not the Russian/Stalinist version) will need to be married to Christianity. The struggle for freedom and a free society, with collective responsibility, will go on. That is why Christianity has such an important role to play. It is not the religion of authority, but the religion of change.

Chapter 9

War and Peace – Violence and Justice

> Actions on behalf of Justice and participation in the transformation of the world fully appear to us as a constitutive dimension of the preaching of the Gospel or in other words, of the Church's mission for the redemption of the human race and its liberation from any oppressive situation.
>
> 1971 World Synod of Catholic Bishops,
> *Justice in the World*

One of the results of the Church becoming the state Church under Constantine was that it abandoned its previously clear policy of opposing war, a move which has had serious consequences right to the present day. At the time of writing, all sections of the Church are still agonising over the outcome of the Gulf crisis. Before the war started, both the Roman Catholic and the Anglican bishops issued statements, but they were not clear declarations of opposition to a war in the Gulf.

They were equivocal. They hedged their positions, getting into deep waters as to whether or not it would be a just war.

The Gulf War

An important correspondence developed in the *Guardian* newspaper on the role of the Church and the possibility of a Gulf war. In one letter, Brian Wicker, Vice-Chairman of Pax Christi, argued that because there is no longer a common military and political culture, St Thomas Aquinas' view is no longer applicable. That is a proposition which I feel may be challenged, but I did agree with him when he said, 'It is unfortunate for Church leaders to appear to be handing over the responsibility to others. They have as much right to pronounce with authority on a proposed "military option" as any general or politician.'

In the debate in the House of Commons on the Gulf crisis in September 1990, I made my position clear, urging negotiations to settle the issue. President Saddam Hussein is a dictator, he has done evil things, such as using gas and chemical weapons against the Kurds in Iraq, and his methods against Iran in the war were not civilised. The unfortunate thing, however, is that the West had, in the past, condoned Saddam's actions. And when attempts had been made to bring the plight of the Kurds in Iraq before the United Nations, the USA had blocked them. The trouble about the attitude of the USA is that it reeks of double standards. For example, in Latin America, it has supported military dictatorships and other reactionary forces, such as the Contras, and in the process has undermined democracy.

It was my view that we should work hard for peace by negotiation without in any way condoning the policies of President Saddam Hussein.

Having said I wanted a peaceful settlement in the Gulf, I want to make it clear that I am not a pacifist. I would have sympathised, for instance, with George Lansbury's position in the 1930s, but I would have argued with him, especially when he believed that Hitler could be persuaded to settle issues without violence.

I agree with Karl Rahner, the Jesuit theologian, when he wrote:

> The principle of the absolute renunciation of force would not . . . be a Christian principle. It would be a heresy which misunderstood the nature of man, his sinfulness and his existence as the interplay of persons in the *one* space of material being. An order of freedom would be misunderstood if it were taken to be an order of things in which force was considered reprehensible on principle.

Jesus and pacifism

It can and will be said that Jesus, in the Sermon on the Mount, was preaching an essentially pacifist doctrine. What he was saying, in fact, was that on certain occasions people who were wrong should be sympathetically judged as to whether on that occasion they should be pardoned.

There are contradictory views shown towards violence in the New Testament. For example, St Paul in Romans, says, 'Never pay back evil for evil . . . If possible . . . live at peace with all men . . . do not seek revenge' (12:17–19). Yet in the same letter he says, 'If you are doing wrong, then you will have cause to fear them [the authorities]; it is not for nothing that they hold the power of the sword . . .' (Romans 13:4).

What is important is that we must, as Christians, promote and defend justice. As Karl Jaspers said,

'There exists amongst men, because they are men, a solidarity through which each shares responsibility for every injustice and every wrong committed in the world . . . If I do not do whatever I can to prevent this, I am an accomplice . . .'

Justice is central to Christ's teaching. As St Augustine said in his *City of God*, 'What are Kingdoms without Justice but large bands of robbers?' In *A Theology of Force and Violence*, Peter Mayhew writes,

> Neither the Bible as a whole, nor the teaching of Jesus in particular, prohibit the use of force. On the other hand, the teaching of Jesus makes it very clear that Governments and Christian people are seriously challenged to think hard before they make the existential decision to use it or support its use. Force may well lead to violence and neither will, of itself, build up the Kingdom of God.

However, Mayhew says there are times when force has to be used, and he quotes Paul Tillich: 'We have to apply force, otherwise . . . we would sacrifice the justice which is the principal form of all social life.'

I fully agree with these views, but each situation must be considered on its merits, and in my view, there is no need to cause a great conflagration in the Middle East by resorting to war. The issue can be solved by negotiation.

Justice in the Middle East

For many years, I was an ardent supporter of Israel. That sprang from the persecution of the Jews by the Nazis, and all of us who were alive and in the armed forces in the war years felt guilty about what the Nazis had done. What we failed to understand was that in opposing an injustice by supporting the state of Israel, we were supporting an injustice against the Palestinian people. As the Israeli state has got older, the conditions of the Palestinians have worsened and the injustice has increased.

In 1968, I led a group of Labour MPs to Israel to see for ourselves what was happening in the occupied territories in the Gaza Strip and the West Bank. I realised then, and said so to the Israeli authorities, that the longer they occupied Gaza and the West Bank, the worse it would get, and in the end the Palestinian people would rise up.

They have now done so. Because of the occupation and oppression they have suffered, can we honestly say they have no right to use some force, as they are doing in their *Intefada* to fight for justice for themselves? They are, in my view, fully justified in their actions, and Christians cannot be against this. Rather we must oppose the Israelis who for years have used force in the Lebanon, in Gaza and the West Bank to ensure that Israel dominates the area.

After what has happened in El Salvador, can we say it is wrong for the guerrillas to use force to fight the government's death squads and the oppression that takes place of the rural and urban poor?

Where dictatorships are in existence, where freedom of speech is destroyed, where violence against the people is carried out daily as it was in Pinochet's Chile, can we, as Christians, say that the people are not right to turn to force to end their misery?

That sort of fight for justice, however, is one thing. Government violence against the people is something else, and no Christian can condone that. State violence, sometimes used in the name of organised Christianity, is unacceptable and must surely be opposed.

Imperialist wars for territory, for oil, for another country's wealth, must also be opposed, as they are against God's will. I believe that to fight Hitler was necessary. As evil as he was, at first it was not quite so easy to judge. It was a growing understanding of his philosophy and actions over a period of time which revealed just how much he had to be fought, and why Christians could in the end give their full support to the war of opposition to him.

Vietnam, Korea and the war against Indonesia were somewhat different. These were imperialist wars of great powers against poor countries, who were accused of being Marxist and Communist. What these peoples were doing was defending themselves and at the same time they wanted to establish their own self-governing states.

Justice in the Soviet Union

Ever since I understood the real nature of the Soviet Union and East European system under Communist control, I gave my support to those who were working for justice in those countries. Obviously, the answer was not military action by the Western governments; in fact, had they resorted to such violence, they would have had to have been opposed. Justice and the fight for it cannot be the reason for double standards. If one rightly supports the fight against the dictatorships in Africa, Asia and Latin America, it is equally important to oppose dictatorships in Eastern or Western Europe. If some of the countries which were, without their agreement, absorbed into the Soviet Union, take action and use force to secure their freedom, then in principle we have no choice but to support them, if the Soviets refuse to grant their independence. As Thomas Merton wrote, 'The theology of love must seek to deal realistically with the evil and injustice in the world and not merely to compromise with them . . . The non-violence ideal does not contain in itself all the answers to all our questions.'

How right that is. As Christians, we must always work for peace, yet there will be times when peace cannot be secured. We should always work for justice, yet justice will not be secured unless some force, or violence, is used.

The world is a complicated place. There are no simple answers to questions, and those who profess simplistic answers to complex issues such as war and peace, justice and injustice, can be dangerous.

The First World War was a very different one from the Second. It was an imperialist war over territories, spheres of influence, industrial raw materials. The Churches in all the countries involved took the side of their governments. British, German, French and Russian troops were blessed by the Church leaders of their own countries, and at no time did the Church leaders condemn the war.

There were, of course, Christian people who did not support the war. They obviously found themselves in difficulties in the Church. There were others who were not Church leaders, but Christians in politics and public life, who fought the war from Day One. Such people as Keir Hardie and George Lansbury and others who were Christians and Socialists came out strongly against the war. Actually, the war broke Keir Hardie's heart and undoubtedly led to his early death. He had hoped that the working people of Europe would have got together and refused to fight against each other, but the reverse was the case.

With the aid of Church leaders, they rallied to their own governments, and for four years allowed the flower of European youth to be destroyed. Lies of a gigantic nature were told. It was said that Christ had appeared in visions in support of the troops of various countries. The propaganda was vile.

Yet despite all, the spirit of Christ did emerge. At the first Christmas the soldiers of parts of the line in

France, both German and British, stopped firing at each other, met, sang Christmas carols and exchanged Christmas greetings on the basis of it being Christ's birthday, with its concept of peace on earth, and goodwill to all men. The rulers of Britain and Germany were horrified. The generals almost went berserk, and as a result those troops involved (on both sides) were broken up, sent to other units and the Christian spirit of goodwill was never allowed to be expressed again.

That getting together in no-man's land was the true spirit of Christianity. It was Christ's preaching being put into practice. Yet instead of the Church leaders welcoming it, they also helped to suppress it. It was both a hopeful and shameful episode. Again, the two trends in Christianity were shown – those who really accepted Christ's teachings, and the rich and powerful, the rulers on both sides, who did not.

Chapter 10

Conclusion

> The primary duty of the Church, not a complementary duty, is the conversion of society. In other words, Christianity is a revolutionary religion or it is nothing.
> Sydney Dark, *The Church, Impotent or Triumphant?*

In this short book I hope I have given some answers to my journalist friend and others who may be interested as to what my Christian beliefs are. I am sure I have not answered all her questions satisfactorily, but I have done my best.

I have explained that my Christianity and belief in God are based on faith. I cannot prove God's existence, but I feel there is a supreme being. The existence of God clearly cannot be scientifically proved, nor can it be disproved, although there are those like the rationalists, the Secular Society, Scientific Socialists, and so on, who would disagree. They say God does not exist, and that's that. I can no longer accept that view.

To me, God means love, that we should love and have

compassion for each other and that we should concern ourselves with the well-being of all. The essence of Christianity is love for our fellow men and women. We should not pass on the other side.

Biased to the poor

I have stressed that Christ's teachings were biased to the poor. The New Testament is full of such evidence. God is on and at their side. Whilst Christ did not advocate the class struggle as such, in practice that is precisely what his teachings added up to.

If that were not the case, why did the ruling class of Israel, in collusion with the Roman authorities, seek to destroy Christ? They did so because he stood for the opposite to what they represented. He was against their oppression and sided with the poor.

There is ample proof to show that the early Church represented the poor, the dispossessed, the unfortunate, the oppressed. This remained the position until the new religion was taken over by the Roman authorities and stood on its head.

I trust, however, that I have not given the impression that Christ was concerned only with the poor. On the contrary, he wanted all to follow him, appealing to all classes and groups and not only to the disadvantaged. I want to stress this because my friend once told me that when she heard me speak at Labour Party conferences, highlighting the struggles and needs of the working class, she felt excluded, as if Socialists like myself did not care about those who are middle class and that our only concern was for the manual workers. She argued that one could hardly build a new society, a new and better world, on that basis. Although she may not have realised it, I was shaken by this, because I really do believe in a classless society, believing that no matter what class people come from, people are people, some good, some bad, and that class origins do not make one a better or worse person. Within all classes in society the individual is all-important, and consistently some people put the interests of society before their own selfish needs.

Certainly, the bias to the poor, the siding with the oppressed and downtrodden, does not mean that Christians can or should exclude or fail to concern themselves with those whose class origins are different. If they did, it would hardly be Christian.

I have stressed that I believe that Christians must be tolerant, understanding of others and compassionate. Whilst the individual is vital and must have freedom to act and think, it is necessary, in order to avoid total anarchy in society, to use the resources of the world for all. Without becoming the bureaucrats of a state-controlled society, state authorities must accept fully the responsibility of helping and concerning themselves with those in need and those who are ill, and the state, by right, should provide the required services.

That is why I believe that the Welfare State, the National Health Service, the right to have a roof over one's head, the provision of a good education, are all basic necessities, and therefore part of Christ's teachings, part of Christ's Kingdom here on earth.

Christians should be positively against war and all forms of racism, which must be combatted. Justice is paramount, and to secure, promote and keep it, it may be necessary at times to use force.

Whilst war must be avoided, this cannot mean that we should always turn the other cheek, as a true pacifist does. Christ's teachings, whilst against war, are not pacifist, although some Christians, referring to biblical texts, would argue the opposite.

Israel 1968

For the first time I revealed that I had a religious experience, a vision, in Israel in 1968, which had a great effect on my life. From that time onwards I again practised my religion, as I had understood it as a child and a young man. I have always had a religious streak in me. Even when an atheist, I was attracted to the Church, but could not explain why. Sometimes I would go to midnight Eucharist or Christmas Day services. It was a contradictory position to find myself in and I have no real explanation for it.

Of course, I always liked High Church services. I loved the singing, the chants, and have always been moved by plainchant as well as the Masses of the great composers.

Yet I never found myself wanting to convert to the Roman Catholic Church, considering myself as a Catholic Anglican. Looking back on the historical event of the break of the Church of England from the Roman Church under Henry VIII, I am appalled at the way in which it was done. I consider myself as part of the universal Church and find I have an affinity with all sections of the Church, both Catholic and Protestant. With regard to Liberation Theology, there are such theologians in both Catholic and Protestant Churches. What they are really doing is applying Christ's teachings to modern society. It is a version of Christianity based firmly on the teachings of the early Church. The interesting thing is that the Christian Socialists were their precursors, and in a sense the first Liberation Theologians.

Throughout Church history there have been those who wanted to get back to Christ's teachings, who rejected the authoritarian, bureaucratic set-up in the Church, and who sought greater democracy and involvement for the laity, especially the poor. It was that desire which caused the religious orders for men and women to be formed, especially the Franciscans, who accepted poverty as a way of life so that they could identify with the early Church's concepts.

There have been great changes in the organisation of the Roman Catholic Church, but still the desire remains for greater involvement of the laity. This has been advocated by theologians such as Hans Küng, who, like Leonardo Boff, have found themselves in trouble with the hierarchy of the Church.

Heaven and Hell

My journalist friend has often put questions to me which I have found some difficulty in answering. I admit I have tended to prevaricate, but in this essay I have been as frank as possible. Yes, I do think there is a God, and that Christ was his son, and that he came to earth through Christ to show us the way forward. On the other hand, I am not sure about heaven, as I do not believe that our life here must be dominated by seeking personal salvation, so that when we die we go comfortably to heaven. I certainly reject the idea of hell. But the old concept of hell, I am glad to say, is no longer accepted by the Roman Church or the Anglican Church, although some of the more extreme Protestant groups still preach 'fire and brimstone'. Such groups, in my opinion, drive people away from the Church and retain only those they have filled with fear.

What will happen to me when I finally die, I cannot be sure and am not greatly concerned. That I am going to die is definite, and it clearly will be sooner rather than later, because of the illness I have which I am informed is incurable; and I trust that when I am taken it will be accepted that I did my best and that I tried to lead as good a life as possible.

There is a mystery about life which is difficult to understand fully. I do believe, however, that there is some design in life. I know that such a view is rejected out of hand by those who are convinced that there is no God, therefore no design, and that we are purely part of the material world, which is in constant evolution.

I certainly accept the evolutionary argument, but in itself that cannot surely be the total answer to life. The mystery unfolds daily, and I believe there is a long way to go before the answer to life is finally, if ever, understood. To work for Christ's Kingdom on earth as it is in heaven, is to give our life a purpose – the purpose of the liberation of mankind. That is why my Socialism and my Christianity are synonymous.

The world is a wonderful place. Daily it gives us happiness. My journalist friend loves the countryside, she is a great walker, goes riding, swims, plays tennis and walks her dog. She lives her life to the full, has a zest and enthusiasm that is a joy to behold. In the course of her activities, together with her husband, she admires the flowers, the trees, the birds, the wild animals, which are there for all of us to enjoy and respect.

The world is integrated. Man is integrated, and our religion is internal as well as external. We are all part of each other, and to create the Kingdom we have to take that concept of our love for each other to the nth degree.

I do not regret the years when I thought I was an atheist and rejected God. In fact, I do not seriously regret much in my life. I could have been kinder to some people, and I am sure I could have had greater understanding and compassion for others.

From the heart

Life has been kind to me. I married a girl of nineteen when I was twenty-four after the war, and we have been together ever since. My wife was never an atheist, but nor was she over-religious. We were married in an Anglican church because both our parents would have been distressed had we not done so. I am glad now that we were, and glad that it was a religious service and that I took the marriage vows, as did my wife. She refused, however, to have the word 'obey' included, and that was as it should be. The full emancipation of women still has to be achieved. Every decade or so the issue arises anew, and today it is clearly before the Church, where women's ordination as priests is an issue that will not go away. The demand for total equality of women is one that will be heard increasingly in the future. Women today do play a fuller part in society as a whole, and it is right that they should.

Leonardo Boff, the great Liberation Theologian, has written a book called *The Maternal Face of God*, which he dedicates 'For my sister and brother, Maria Lina and Clodovis, of the Order of the Servants of Mary, that they may succeed in living the spirit of the Magnificat'. Beneath his dedication he quotes John Paul I: 'God is Father, but especially, Mother.' That really says it all. It is the acceptance that God is part of us, and that we are part of God, irrespective of sex, race or religion.

Father Boff makes the point in his book that the Marian texts of the Bible are 'very important'. He says, 'They contain God's message for us . . . We hear a voice that speaks to our ears of today.'

Further, he says, 'Biblical meaning of course cannot be altogether fixed or frozen in the past . . . The interpretation of a text is always a two-way street then. Sacred Scripture is not a cistern of stagnant water, in which all legitimate meanings lie submerged and 'ready to go'. Sacred Scripture is a fountain of fresh, living water, from which new meanings emanate in light of the times in which we live, suffer and seek meaning.' For me, Father Boff has got it absolutely right.

I have often said to my journalist friend that God gave us free will. I am sure she will exercise hers when considering what I have written. I only wish it were more learned, but it is what I believe, and I trust it will help solve any doubts she may still have.

Appendix I

John Wheatley MP

Lecture delivered at St Margaret's Church, Westminster
by Eric Heffer MP, 1st March 1989

Mankind, we understand, is made in the image of God. Man, and woman therefore, are central to Christianity. It should be remembered that Christ was crucified as the Son of God, who, because of his support for the poor, was in conflict with the establishment of his day.

As Archbishop Helder Camara said to his diocese when he became Archbishop of Olinda and Recife in Brazil in April 1964, 'I must have special love, like Christ, for the poor. At the last judgement, we shall all be judged by our treatment of Christ, of Christ who hungers and thirsts, who is dirty, injured and oppressed.' He went on to say, 'We are all convinced that freedom is a divine gift which must be preserved at any price. Let us liberate, in the fullest sense of the word, every human creature in our midst.'

In a real sense, the concept of Liberation Theology was clearly being spelt out by the archbishop.

Father Gustavo Gutierrez, a priest from a poor background and a pioneer of Liberation Theology, wrote eight important works which were published as *The Power of the Poor in History*, in which he said: 'We support the aspirations of labourers and peasants, who wish to be treated as free, responsible human beings. They are called to share in the decisions that affect their lives and their future.'

Before the concept was developed by modern theologians, John Wheatley, in his own way, was preaching and advocating Liberation Theology. He was from the poor, and all his adult life, both as a Christian and then a Socialist, he worked unceasingly for the poor. He believed in the Socialist revolution, non-violent, but a revolution nonetheless. He was a bold, courageous man, who was not only prepared to stand against the political establishment of his day, but equally found himself in conflict with some of the hierarchy in his own Church. He felt that God's Kingdom should be created here on earth.

John Wheatley was born into a Roman Catholic family in the County of Waterford in southern Ireland, thirty years after the great famine, in 1869. His father, Thomas Wheatley, was desperately poor, an agricultural labourer, and in 1873, he, his wife and four children, the eldest being John, left Ireland for Scotland, where he worked as a miner in the Lanarkshire coalfields. The Wheatleys lived in a one-roomed, back-to-back house. The floor of the house was stone, there was neither drainage nor water supply and the tenants had to get their water from a common tap a hundred yards away. The lavatory was an ash pit which served twelve families. It faced the windows of the row of houses and an open sewer ran in front of the houses.

All his life John Wheatley was, one might say, obsessed with housing for the poor, and one can understand why. John went to school at the St Bridget Chapel School at Bailliestane, but economic necessity forced him to leave school and go down the mines at the age of thirteen. Those were harsh days for the miners, and just about three years after starting work, the mine-owners successfully reduced the men's wages from three shillings and sixpence a day to two shillings and sixpence a day.

John Wheatley was undoubtedly influenced by

Michael Davitt, a leader of the Irish National League. Davitt, against the advice of the League, had supported Keir Hardie in the 1888 General Election. He had founded the Land League of Ireland in 1879, and consistently fought against tenant evictions.

John Wheatley was first an Irish Nationalist, but circumstances and events turned him towards Socialism. It was the principles of Socialism that caught his imagination, not the name. Socialism was for the poor. It would be a society which got rid of poverty. It would give real freedom to the oppressed, and that idea clearly fitted in with his understanding of Christianity.

Wheatley was thirty-six years old when he became a Socialist. Having become a Socialist, he felt he had to convert his fellow working-class Roman Catholics to the Socialist cause, and he had a letter published in the *Glasgow Observer* of 24th February 1906 headed 'A Catholic Defence of Socialism'. John Hannon, in his book *The Life of John Wheatley*, says, 'It was a condemnation of the Capitalist system which he said made it impossible for Catholics to practise their religion and therefore it was incumbent on them to fight against it – "Living in a society which is one of the swindler versus the swindled, how can there be brotherly love?"'

This led to quite a furore in the Church. John Wheatley was bitterly attacked by some of the clergy, including some in the hierarchy, but being Wheatley, he did not take it lying down. In a reply in the *Glasgow Observer* on 10th March 1906, he in turn attacked the clergy, who, he argued, had failed to fight consistently against poverty. He said to them, 'Step aside and let the workers have a go.' He said they should not take the side of the oppressors: 'Do not keep the company of the oppressor for in the smoke of battle, you may well be taken for one of them.' How clearly that is in line with Christ's views when he drove the moneylenders and merchants out of the Temple.

At the end of 1906, an advertisement appeared in the *Glasgow Observer*, urging Roman Catholics who were interested in Socialism to go to a meeting at the College Street Halls in Glasgow. It is interesting to note that Catholics from every walk of life responded to that call. George Hardie, brother of Keir Hardie, attended and spoke, and out of it was formed the Catholic Socialist Society. Wheatley became President, and Stephen Pullman its Secretary.

Protestants were unhappy with what Wheatley had done, but Wheatley, from the word go, set his sights against sectarianism. For example, in the summer of 1907 he wrote to the *Glasgow Observer* urging Catholics and Irish working-men to vote for John Stewart, the non-Catholic Labour candidate. He wrote, 'Do not be used or sacrificed by men coming forward to avenge imaginary grievances. Your interests and those of your fellow Protestant workers are identical. Your enemies are their enemies. Workers of every creed unite.'

Today, in Latin America, where Liberation Theology began, there are Liberation Theologians who are Catholic and Protestant. They are echoing what Wheatley first argued in 1906.

John Wheatley, because he identified himself with the poor, argued strongly for class politics. He was, in fact, arguing as the prophet Amos did. Amos argued that the rich of his day used every known means of fraud and deception in measures, weights and goods. They defrauded the poor of their wages and worked them without mercy. He said that the lesson to draw is that the earth can be made a foretaste of paradise or a hell, accordingly as religion is followed, or its counsels are cast to the wind.

As I said earlier, Wheatley was ahead of his time. He saw things very clearly indeed, and this is particularly borne out in his attitude to Marxism. In an article in the

Book of the Labour Party, vol. 3, 1925, he wrote in 'Why a Labour Party?':

> To me it seems that the ideal of Marx was to emancipate the common people from the exploitation of those who owned the means of life. He argued that in every stage the owning class exploited those who were compelled to work for wages, and the nature of the clashings was not spiritual or moral but economic. He suggested as a remedy that the 'workers of the world should unite' to strike the fetters from their limbs in order to attain to a condition of freedom. There seems nothing unbeautiful about this, nor anything antagonistic to the ideals of those who have dreamed of a better system of society.

Many years after John Wheatley had said this, the French Catholic philosopher and theologian Teilhard de Chardin, wrote in a letter in June 1952: 'As I like to say, the synthesis of the Christian God Above and the Marxist God Ahead is the only God whom we can henceforth adore in spirit and in truth.'

Father Teilhard de Chardin, like Wheatley, was not a timid man. He did not seek to turn Christians away from the real world, from the militant world, from human effort in that world. He did not belittle what the people of the world were doing. On the contrary, he magnified and exalted them and therefore integrates them in his synthesis. His book *The Phenomenon of Man* was in my opinion one of the most important books written and produced this century.

John Wheatley did not have the opportunity to read and study the works of this priest but in his own way he trod the same path, and for that alone he should be revered and accepted as someone who was a reflection of God.

John Wheatley, after leaving the coalmines became a public house manager. Later, he created a business. He was successful as a businessman, but he never forgot his roots, and where he came from. To Wheatley, work for the poor, the oppressed, the downtrodden, the working class, was all-important.

He was the most, some would say the only, successful Minister in the 1924 Labour government. His Housing Act was the best thing to come out of that government. John Wheatley, as I said earlier, was deeply concerned about housing for working-class people. He was one of those who led the great Rent Strike in Glasgow in 1915. He became Chairman of the Glasgow Labour Party Housing Conference. He argued for cottages for the workers and at the May Day Rally urged the landlords not to increase rents. The landlords, being landlords, refused to take any notice of what was being said. Neilson and Sons of Buchan Street, a very large landlord, decided to put up rents from an average of thirteen shillings to twenty-four shillings per annum. That was the second increase the tenants had had since the beginning of the war. Immediately, the Women's Housing Association organised a protest.

All over the city, workers got involved in a struggle against rent increases. In September some workers took strike action. The action of the rent strikers and the factory workers was successful.

John Wheatley was elected to Parliament for Shettleston, Glasgow, in 1922, and in 1924 became a Cabinet Minister of Health. He then got down to the task of building houses for working people. He brought in his Housing Act, which involved the Trade Unions and local authorities. Under that Act, 500,000 houses for working people were built. It was a tremendous achievement.

Like Christ, Wheatley was unwavering in his support for working people. He did not compromise with his principles. One of the most important things for him was that working people should have decent houses to live in. He would have roundly approved of the Church of England's *Faith in the City*.

Today, we still have terrible housing problems, and the words of John Wheatley in Hansard of 24th March 1923 are as apposite now as they were then. He said in a speech: 'The problem is not one of house building, but of finance. It is part and parcel of the great social problem by which at every step we are baffled by poverty at the one end and exploitation at the other. I speak as one of many people on this side of the House who has studied the housing problem from hard experience of living in the slums.' Wheatley believed that by building houses, the unemployment problem could also be tackled.

It could be argued that he was not the type to be a saint. He was a family man, a public house keepers a businessman, an MP. I take the view that if it is accepted that a saint is close to God and accessible to man, then John Wheatley had all the attributes of saintliness. I believe that John Wheatley was close to God and he was accessible to man. He was, in my view, doing God's work here on earth. He made mistakes. He was misunderstood, as he was on issues like birth control. (As a Catholic he was accepting his Church's teaching, but he felt the answer for working people was to provide houses for them.) But he was always accessible and he dedicated his life to the poor.

His nephew, Lord Wheatley, Tam Dalyell's late father-in-law, made this point in his book *One Man's Judgement*. He said of his Uncle John: 'Along with others, including my father, he founded the Catholic Socialist Society, which existed for a number of years until the battle was won . . . The important fact is that the Wheatley brothers, John and Patrick, and a number of others who took that stand, fought the battle within the Church and remained faithful to their religion . . .'

That in a sense says it all. Let us all say Amen to that.

Appendix II

Socialism and the Church: The Lessons are There

Published in *The Times*, 10th April 1978

It has been said that the Church of England is the Tory Party at prayer. Mrs Thatcher's view is that historically it is nearer the mark to say that the Tory Party in its origin was the Church of England in politics. Certainly many Tories would like that to be the case.

My thoughts have turned to the question of religion and politics because of Mrs Thatcher's recent speech at St Lawrence Jewry Church in the City of London. Her theme was Christian society and how it should apply to Britain. At least Jim Callaghan will take comfort from knowing that Mrs Thatcher does not regard her political opponents as being devils, although she may consider the left wing of the Labour Party as being in that category.

It is true that over the years the Church of England and certain Tories have been closely connected. They still are, and it is they in particular who argue most fiercely that the Church should 'keep out of politics', as if the Church had never been involved in politics. The Church of England is the Established Church, and that position has not been developed and maintained without political persecution. Even today, although happily not too often, Church of England matters come before Parliament and debates and votes take place on Church issues.

The struggles within the Church, the compromise of

the Thirty-Nine Articles with its delicate balance between Catholic and Protestant theological concepts, the rise of Protestantism, the splits and division in the Church were all, in their own way, political events. The English civil war was largely fought out in religious terms, yet it was really about the transference of power from one class to another, and nothing could be more political than that.

To underline the religious nature of politics at the time of the English civil war which led to parliamentary power, it is interesting to note that between 1649 and 1660 Westminster Hall was used by booksellers who flooded their bookstalls with pamphlets from the Presbyterians, Independents, Anabaptists and Levellers. It is estimated that between 1640 and 1659 more than 32,000 such publications saw the light of day. It cannot therefore be said that politics and religion did not have a clear connection in those days.

It can be said that the basis of Socialist thinking lies in Christianity. I realise such a statement will produce howls of anguish from some Conservative politicians as well as the sectarian left in politics, but facts are facts. The early Christians were regarded as subversives and persecuted by Rome before Christianity became synonymous with Roman power. It should not be forgotten that Jesus himself was regarded both as a heretic and a subversive who spent his life fighting the establishment, never coming to terms with it.

In Britain, in the middle ages, every priest did not support the establishment, as evidenced by the activities of the so-called hedge priests such as John Ball who threw in his lot with Wat Tyler during the 1381 Peasants' Revolt. Christianity has, since its inception, had both a progressive and reactionary side to it, and it is no good politicians claiming that Christianity supports their particular views.

A Socialist can support his claim that Christianity is

basically Socialist by quoting some of the early Christian fathers. St Ambrose, for example, commenting on Christ's reference to birds who did not produce thrift by storing food into barns, said: 'They are a good example, truly, and are worthy of our faithful imitation, for if God's providence never fails to supply the fowls of Heaven, albeit they use no husbandry, and trouble nothing about the prospects of the harvest, the true cause of our want would seem to be avarice. It is for this reason that they have an abundance of suitable victuals, because they have not learnt to claim as their private and peculiar property the fruits of the earth, which have been given to them in common for their food. We have lost common property by the claims of private property.' He further said, 'The land was made for all, why do ye rich men claim it as your private property?'

St Gregory the Great, who was mainly responsible for the conversion of England to Christianity, said of rich men, 'We must make them clearly understand that the land which yields them income is the common property for all men, and for this reason the fruits of it which are brought forth are for the common welfare.'

I could give many other quotations from the early Christian fathers, but I give only one more and that is from the formula of the Nicean Council. That council was accepted as final by the Eastern Orthodox and Anglican communions and is regarded as infallible by the Roman Catholic Church. It says: 'We look for a new heaven and a new earth, when there shall have shone the appearing and kingdom of the great God, and our Saviour Jesus Christ; and then as Daniel saith, the saints of the Most High shall take the Kingdom. And the earth shall be pure, holy, the earth of the living, and not of the dead (which David foreseeing with the eye of faith, exclaims, I believe verily to see the goodness of the Lord in the land of the living), the earth of the gentle and lowly. For blessed, saith the Lord, are the meek, for they shall inherit the earth: and the prophet saith, the feet of the poor and needy shall tread it.'

There have long been groups in the Church of England who have identified themselves with Socialism. The first such group was headed by the Reverend Frederick Denison Maurice and Charles Kingsley. In 1849, Kingsley, speaking at a meeting, declared, 'I am a Church of England clergyman, and I am a Chartist.' F. D. Maurice also said, 'Competition is put forth as the law of the universe. That is a lie. The time has come for us to declare that it is a lie by word and by deed.'

Later, in 1877 Stewart Headlam, then a London curate, founded the Guild of St Matthew. In 1888 the guild presented their views to the Pan-Anglican Conference of Bishops. They said, 'Our present social system – if the words "social system" can be used of that which is largely the outcome of anarchic competition – is cruel and dishonest, and needs drastic reform and radical reorganisation .' At the end of their statement the guild said, 'with the main contentions of the Socialist, the Christian is not only able but bound to agree.'

The Labour Party has always contained a Christian element as well as a Marxist one. The two have often overlapped in the same individual, as instanced by Mervyn Stockwood's recent book *The Cross and the Sickle.* Some of its left-wing leaders in the past, such as George Lansbury, were Christians and during their lifetime were attacked as subversives, Marxists, agitators, Leninists, etc.

In 1926, during the general strike, *Lansbury's Bulletin* said, 'Tomorrow is Sunday. You will come to our meetings at night, but I would like you to attend the Church service nearest your home . . . It is Christ's gospel of passive resistance you are practising today.'

One can see, therefore, from the above quotations that it is impossible for Tories to claim that they alone are in the Christian tradition and that their ideas are in line with Christian teaching.

It is true that in arguing the way she did in her 'sermon', Mrs Thatcher was in line with some of the views held by some of the early Christians. For example, Hilary of Pocitina said, 'To possess riches is not wrongful, but rather the manner in which possession is used.' It is interesting to note that Hilary was not concerned with the manner in which the possessions were accumulated.

The business concepts which attached themselves to Christianity were developed side by side with the rise of Protestantism, especially Calvinism. The doctrine of predestination counteracted the type of brooding anxiety of spirit, which it was felt at times was apt to sap the energy which would otherwise be available for money-making. As J. A. Hobson puts it in his book *God and Mammon*, 'Above all, disregarding the express teaching of Christ about the dangers of riches, it regarded these with favour as the natural fruit of business ingenuity and toil, condemning only their misuse for self-indulgence and ostentation.' In other words, the idea of getting wealth at the expense of others is perfectly all right, but one must not reveal the ugly face of capitalism in the process.

The argument that Christianity is synonymous with capitalism is as false as the argument that capitalism means liberty and freedom. The truth is that the aim of Socialists, like that of the early Christians, is the creation of the Brotherhood of Man. Unfortunately, over the years, that phrase has too often been mouthed by slick politicians who have debased its true meaning. Socialism, like Christianity, must convince people that it has a great impersonal objective which would give meaning and dignity to their lives.

William Morris summed up the true Socialist concept when he wrote, 'For fellowship is heaven, and lack of fellowship is hell: fellowship is life, and lack of fellowship is death: and the deeds that ye do upon the earth, it is for fellowship sake that ye do them, and the life that is in it, that shall live on for ever and ever, and each one of you are part of it, while many a man's life upon the earth from the earth shall wane.'

Appendix III

Moral Values

Speech made in the House of Commons,
13th February 1989

I welcome the fact that we are discussing this matter today. Although the Hon. Member for Bromsgrove (Sir H. Miller) has been moderate – I appreciate the fact that he says that he comes from a Christian Socialist background – unfortunately some of his colleagues, including some of his Hon. Friends, still consider the Church of England to be the Tory party at prayer. They believe that politics should be left to Tory politicians and that only they have the right to be concerned with such matters. They believe that the Church of England should be concerned only with the saving of individual souls.

Their objective is either to maintain the status quo – as long as that equates with the present economic capitalist system – or, if changes are to take place, to remove the welfare state, trade union rights, the National Health Service, council house building and local authority rights in the interests of business, especially big business.

As somebody who was born into the Church – I am sure that I will die a member of the Church – I am passionately concerned with the interests of my Church. I believe that the Church has a right to involve itself in politics. Indeed, it has a duty to do so. The politics of the Church should be the politics of the early

Christians. As Bishop Sheppard of Liverpool said in his book, there should be a 'Bias to the Poor'.

The Hon. Member for Bromsgrove referred to Archbishop William Temple who said – I agree with him – that Christianity must

> criticise actual institutions in the light of its own social principles, because it aims, not at the salvation of individuals one by one, but at that perfect individual and social welfare, which is called the Kingdom of God or the Holy City.

The arguments that we shall hear today against the bishops – we hear them regularly from Conservative Members – were used against Archbishop Temple in the past. I would like to draw the attention of the House to the fact that in 1934 William Temple wrote to *The Times* urging Neville Chamberlain, then Chancellor of the Exchequer, not to decrease income tax but to restore cuts which had been made in unemployment benefit. Neville Chamberlain was furious. That is perhaps a mild word to use. He was absolutely mad. He wrote to *The Times*:

> When I read that letter I thought it was a pity that the Archbishop should suggest, as it seems to me he did by implication, that MPs require to be reminded of humanitarian feelings which otherwise would not occur to them.

The archbishop was right to send his letter. Members of Parliament, certainly some in the House today, have to be reminded of humanitarian feelings. If Christians are not genuinely concerned with the spiritual welfare of people, they must be concerned with the material needs of people. There is no contradiction in that.

Let me recall again the words of the Magnificat. It is much more revolutionary in some senses than the Communist manifesto. The Magnificat reads:

> He hath shewed strength with his arm; he hath scattered the proud in the imagination of their hearts.
>
> He hath put down the mighty from their seats, and exalted them of low degree.
>
> He hath filled the hungry with good things; and the rich he hath sent empty away.

That does not fit in with some of the concepts which Tory Members may accept.

There was an interesting and great Roman Catholic professor of political economy of the university of Naples in 1890 who said in his book on Christian Socialism:

> According to St Jerome, opulence is always the result of theft, if not committed by the actual possessor, then by his predecessors.

That is not much different from what many Socialists have said in the past. I believe that to be true.

We should also remember that Acts 4:32 states that the members of the first Christian communities were

> of one heart and of one soul, neither said any of them that aught of the things he possessed was his own, but they had all things in common.

St Cyprea in *Of Works and Arms* said:

> When at the first beginnings of the Church the mind flourished with great virtues, when the soul of the believers burned with a glow of faith yet new, then they had all things common, they initiated the divine law, the equality of God the Father.

I believe that. That was why I am both a Christian and a Socialist. I do not find that the concepts I hold as a

Socialist are any different from the beliefs I was brought up with.

Many Tory Members have got away from the basic concepts of the Christian Church. They have forgotten how it started and what it is about. It is true that at some stage it became the state religion, so turned into its opposite, like Marxism in Russia. It, too, became the opposite of what it began as. That is not new – unfortunately, it happens too often – but that does not mean that those who began the process – the early Christians and early Socialists – were wrong. It means that those who came afterwards distorted what those who began the process believed. That is what I have always thought. I see no difference between the two, and I find it difficult to understand the arguments of some Tory Members.

I do not disagree with what the Church has been doing recently. In the past I have been a critic of our bishops. Their report on the bomb was excellent. I am only sad that the Synod has overturned it. Fair enough, that is a democratic decision. I fully agree with chapter 3 of *Faith in the City* which deals with theological priorities. Paragraph 3.3 states:

> In this country we are confronted by an acute form of relative poverty – officially recognised as 'multiple deprivation' – that is particularly concentrated in the Urban Priority Areas, and that is caused to a great extent by circumstances beyond the control of those affected by it. There is a clear Christian duty to respond to this situation and 'remember the poor' in our urban priority areas.

Can anybody disagree with that?

The report continues:

> It is against the background of the excessive individualism of much Christian thinking in the nineteenth century

> that we must place Marx's perception that evil is to be found, not just in the human heart, but in the very structures of economic and social relationships. This perception is also found to a notable degree in the Old Testament [from which . . . Marx may have derived it] where there is explicit recognition of the inevitable tendency of the rich to get richer and the poor poorer unless some constraint is imposed to limit the freedom of individuals to profit without restraint from a market economy.

That is the right approach for my Church.

Today in Latin America, Asia and Africa there is a growth in what is called Liberation Theology. *Faith in the City* states:

> To all of us, the example of Liberation Theology opens up the possibility that new priorities, as well as new methods, can restore to us a theology that is truly relevant to the needs and aspirations of people today. Therefore we have to apply the new theology to the situation that exists in Britain today.

I accept that. We cannot talk about Liberation Theology only in Latin America. Hon. Members who saw last night's programme about the Sudan will have been made ill. Everyone who is a genuine Christian must have felt sick, seeing the poverty and misery that exists in the Sudan, Ethiopia, Latin America and various parts of Asia.

What about our poverty? We cannot act to solve the problem too quickly. We are a rich nation. What about our poverty? We have to do something about it. Therefore, I agree with *Faith in the City* that we must concern ourselves equally with what is happening in our own country.

One example is housing. When I think of the Government's record and policy on housing, and of the needs of our people, I remember what the report says about housing. In the section headed 'Public Housing: the Way Forward', paragraph 10.72 on page 250 states:

> The great importance of the public housing ideal was that it broke the link between poverty and living conditions. The poor did not have to live in poor housing. But this link is now being re-established . . . Net capital spending was cut by 44 per cent in volume terms between 1975–76 and 1979–80 and by 52 per cent in cash terms between 1979–80 and 1984–85. The result is that the number of new homes started in the public sector has dropped over the last decade from 174,000 in 1975 to 38,000 in 1984. At the same time there has been a shift in expenditure away from the metropolitan districts and London in favour of the shire districts.

In the conclusion to the chapter on housing, the report states:

> What is beyond dispute we believe is that a continuing emphasis upon home ownership alone will not solve the housing problems of the urban priority areas.

That is Liberation Theology as argued by the Church in Britain, and I believe that it is absolutely right.

Mr Ian Gow (Eastbourne): The passage which the Hon. Gentleman, perfectly understandably, has just read to the House is the best illustration that one could find of where the Church – the best motives – is commenting upon matters that are very much within the judgment and responsibility of politicians, whether at local or at national level. Some of us would have been much happier if *Faith in the City* had directed its attention to saving the souls of the people rather than making political judgments on how housing might be improved.

Mr Heffer: I am delighted that the Hon. Gentleman said that, because he has made my point for me. If they want to save souls, they had better house the people properly. If they want to save souls, they had better give the people decent jobs and full employment. If they want to save souls, they had better become concerned with personal relationships and what is happening at home. That is what Christianity and Socialism are about. The Hon. Gentleman has attacked the report, just as some of his Hon. Friends have attacked the bishops, precisely because they have asked vital questions that are apposite to the needs of the people. I believe that the Church has come down, rightly, on the side of doing something about the problems.

In his book *Essays on Christian Politics and Kindred Subjects*, William Temple said:

> It is not possible to limit Christianity to the individual alone. Christianity appeared in the world as a society. It was not indeed a society with a finished constitution presenting what officers it should have, or what its specific aims should be.

I agree with that.

Unlike some people in Muslim and other countries, I do not believe that Christians want to have a theocratic state. I do not agree with the Christian Democrats in Europe, who wish to involve themselves in political affairs and say, 'This is what we shall impose on society.' The Hon. Member for Eastbourne (Mr Gow) is as good a Christian as I am. I accept that people who have different political views are sincere Christians. We may argue about our interpretation of Christianity, but I do not want us as Christians to say that we shall impose our views on other people. I am sure that most other Hon. Members will accept that. It is a question of our basic ideals of Christianity.

Dame Elaine Kellett-Bowman: Does the Hon. Gentleman agree that one of the basic ideals of Christianity is that there should be one man and one woman for life?

Mr Heffer: I do not argue with that. I have done rather well in that regard. But I believe that Christians should have compassion and understanding for people who may move in different directions from ourselves. When Conservative Members have strayed, I have been asked by the press for my views. I have said that it is a matter for them, not for me to sit in judgment. I am not God and I do not pretend to have Godlike powers. I look to him to help me to come to my views on issues, but I do not sit easily in judgment on other people. One great problem is with people who suddenly find morality. That does not relate to the basic concepts of Christianity.

The Church has gone through many evolutionary phases. At times, it has become the opposite of what was intended. It began as the society of the poor. Later, it was transformed into the religion of the state, and it became all-powerful. A powerful universal state within states was defined by those who wanted to get back to its original principles. During the middle ages, a feeling developed that Christianity should be the poor man's charter. That feeling became the chief contributory cause of the rise of all the movements, whether they were Catholic or supposedly heretical, Franciscan or Waldensian, which were in being from the thirteenth century onwards. In Britain they were embodied in the ideas of Wycliffe and, in a practical way, in the Peasants' Revolt of 1381. Troelsch, who studied these movements, was led to describe the period of the later middle ages as the '*Laiechristentum*' – the time of the common man's Christianity.

Political struggles and involvement have been endemic in Christianity from the very beginning, and whether some like it or not, that is still the case today. The rise of Protestantism was part of the struggle for political freedom, for democracy and for the right to speak freely, which is now accepted by most Christians, no matter to which branch of the faith they belong.

The Church has a number of currents within it, the basic concept being the creation of God's Kingdom on earth and the need to create a society where things are owned in common and where people act together for the commonweal. At the same time, individuals have rights and minds of their own, and they must be given every facility to use them. That is the important point about Christianity. We were given free will. We must use that free will for the benefit of the mass of the ordinary people in society – the poor and the oppressed. I believe that the individual's rights must be part of the collective whole. Those rights, together with the obligations, must be accepted by all.

I shall read extracts from two poems which I believe are essential in understanding why the Church and Christianity must be involved in politics. George Lovelace, the leader of the Tolpuddle martyrs, was a Methodist preacher. I have never been a Methodist, although my mother-in-law is one. After seven years' transportation, which was, as it were, given to him by the state at that time, he responded with a poem, 'God is Our Guide':

God is our guide, from field, from wave,
From plough, from anvil, and from loom:
We came, our country's rights to save,
And speak a tyrant factor's doom:
We raise the watchword liberty;
We will, we will, we will be free.

God is our guide! No swords we draw.
We kindle not war's battle fires.
By reason, union, justice, law,
We claim the birthright of our sires;
We raise the watchword, liberty,
We will, we will, we will be free!!!

George Lovelace was concerned about the morals of his children. He wrote to his wife Betsy:

Be satisfied, my dear Betsy, on my account. Depend on it, it will work together for good and we shall yet rejoice together. I hope you will pay particular attention to the morals and spiritual interest of the children. Don't send me any money to distress yourself. I shall do well, for He who is the Lord of the winds and waves will be my support in life and death.

I shall now read from the hymn or poem, however one looks at it, 'Jerusalem' by Blake. It is something which we all sing with fervour in our churches and in our meetings. We must think about what it means:

And did those feet in ancient time
Walk upon England's mountains green?
And was the Holy Lamb of God
On England's pleasant pastures seen?
And did the countenance divine
Shine forth upon our clouded hills?
And was Jerusalem builded here
Among these dark satanic mills?

Bring me my bow of burning gold!
Bring me my arrows of desire!
Bring me my spear! O clouds, unfold!
Bring me my chariot of fire!
I will not cease from mental fight,

Nor shall my sword sleep in my hand,
Till we have built Jerusalem
In England's green and pleasant land.

That is what I believe. I believe that Christianity is about transforming society to make it better. The Church must be involved in politics. It must concern itself with what is happening around us. It must become up to date. If it has to decide on such issues as whether there should be women priests and whether those who are divorced should hold positions in the Church, it is because it must live in modern society. It does not mean that the basic concept is wrong, but that we must accept that the Church must be involved. If it is not involved, it cannot make the contribution that it should in building a new society – in building that Jerusalem – and creating a new world. That is what I believe, and that is why I became involved in this debate.